A GUIDE TO FEEDING
HORSES AND PONIES

PELHAM HORSEMASTER SERIES

A GUIDE TO FEEDING HORSES AND PONIES

A. C. Leighton Hardman

PELHAM BOOKS
LONDON

First published in Great Britain by Pelham Books Ltd
44 Bedford Square, London WC1B 3DP
1977
Reprinted 1980 and 1983
This paperback edition published 1985

British Library Cataloguing in Publication Data

Leighton Hardman, A. C.
  A guide to feeding horses and ponies. – 2nd ed.
  – (Pelham horsemaster series)
  1. Horses–Feeding and feeds
  I. Title
  632.61'084   SF285.5

  ISBN 0 7207 1577 6

Typeset by Allset Composition
Printed in Great Britain by Hollen Street Press, Slough and
bound by Hunter and Foulis, Edinburgh

Contents

Foreword

By Lieutenant Colonel C. R. D. Gray
(Former Director of The National Stud)

This book is more than a guide to feeding — it is almost a bible — containing as it does so much knowledge, both scientific and practical, in the art of feeding horses.

It should be of great help to every person who really wants to learn the basic principles of feeding and, for the veterinary or agricultural student, it would seem to be essential reading in this field.

The author has made a thorough study of her subject and has wisely sought the guidance of many eminent horsemen and veterinarians in the writing of the book which is the first of its kind to be published in the British Isles.

Douglas Gray.

Newmarket 1977

Acknowledgments

I wish to say how much I appreciate the help I have received in writing this book, especially from Mr G. H. Francis, BSc; and Mr J. H. Murray NDA, nutritional adviser with Peter Hand (GB) Ltd; also Messrs G. Hall and Ian Mackie of R.H.M. Ltd, Wimborne, Dorset; members of the staff of Spillers Ltd, including Dr Graham Chapman and Dr David Frape who assisted me with the digestion diagrams. Sidney Ricketts, BSc, FRCVS, for correcting the chapter on disease conditions and also advising and helping me in other respects; Mr G. Allsup; and last but by no means least I wish to thank Dr W. R. Cook for his advice on respiratory problems.

Newmarket
February 1980
A.C.L.H.

Introduction

Feeding horses has always been a matter of tradition;
the skills acquired over hundreds of years were passed
down by the older stud grooms to the boys who worked
under them for most of their lives. Basically these
grooms knew what best to give the horses but scientifically they could not know exactly why they were doing
certain things; they just knew when their horses looked
right.

In 'the good old days', when the horse was largely
cared for by professionals, the overall standard of
management throughout the country was, in all proba-
bility, higher than it tends to be today. Recognising this
problem, some of the major manufacturers of animal
foodstuffs, starting in the late 1950s, decided to market
a complete range of horse and pony rations to assist
both the professional and the amateur horse owner
and so enable everyone to feed a correctly balanced
'modern' ration.

Until very recently, the only scientific research
carried out on nutrition was the work done on ruminants — rightly or wrongly this was applied to horses.
With the ever-increasing interest in amateur riding, it has
now become economically possible and fashionable to
devote both time and money to research into equine
nutrition.

If only for the sake of the horse or pony, every owner
should know the basic principles of feeding if he intends
to feed nothing but cubes. In this book I have tried
to outline these basic principles as a guide to the more

9

enlightened feeding of horses and ponies, and as far as possible have explained the reasons why we should or should not do certain things.

1: Equipment Used for Feeding and Watering

As food for horses and ponies is now such an expensive item, wastage must be reduced to a minimum. Mice usually present the greatest problem where food is stored in sacks for any length of time, for not only do they waste food by making holes in the sacks but they also contaminate it with their excreta. A stable cat will help but the final answer is to keep all the food in mouse-proof storage bins, the size of bins required depending on the number of horses kept.

If you own only one or two horses, ordinary metal or plastic household dustbins are quite satisfactory provided they have lids, but if a larger number of horses is to be catered for, purpose-built metal feed-storage bins (see Fig. 1) should be used.

These bins will also provide you with a means of storing a quantity of whole grain and enable you to buy in bulk at a more realistic price — linseed, for example, will keep well for about a year or so in a bin and this will work out at a fraction of the cost of buying a few pounds at a time throughout the year.

Linseed must be boiled before it is fed to horses (see Chapter 13); in small quantities this can be done in a saucepan first on top of a stove and then simmered in a slow oven; larger quantities can be cooked in a domestic clothes boiler but have a tendency to fuse, particularly when barley is being boiled with linseed, in which case it is better to suspend a bucket containing the food inside the boiler, which is filled with water. Special linseed boilers are available, and work either on the

11

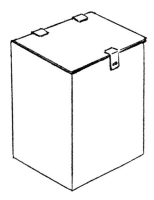

Fig. 1 Purpose-built metal feed-storage bin

percolator or water-jacket principle and can be regulated to simmer quietly for several hours without boiling over.

Large stables will probably find it cheaper to buy whole oats in bulk and keep them loose in a vermin-proof loft, or in hessian sacks or grain bins; in the latter case, it is preferable to have two bins rather than one as when new grain is added to a partly filled bin, it will tend to flow down the middle of the bin, leaving the older grain around the sides. Bins should be emptied completely before they are re-filled. The grain is usually transported from the loft or bins by means of a grain auger, to an oat crusher as required.

Mite-infested or rancid grain can cause digestive upsets when fed to animals, therefore great care must be taken to keep all storage bins clean and dry. Whole grain with an initial moisture content of not more than 16 per cent will usually store well if kept in a dry and well-ventilated building. Whole grain for storage in bins should be drier than grain for storage in sacks. Once crushed, however, its keeping time is reduced to between two and four weeks depending on the weather. Old food should be used up completely and feed bins swept out before any new food is added, otherwise over a period of time mites may appear. Mite-infested food has a very characteristic smell and a fine dust can usually be seen. If the dust is examined under a low-powered microscope, the mites can be observed; even without the aid of a microscope it is sometimes possible to see the dust moving around. The bins will then have to be cleaned out carefully and fumigated before they are used again.

When loose food is placed on the ground for horses to eat, a large portion of it is often lost, as many horses have a natural instinct to paw at the ground while they are eating. In doing so they can scatter their food over a large area, mixing it with their bedding or losing it in the surrounding grass. Therefore proper food receptacles should be used and placed above ground level or made with a sufficiently wide base so that they cannot be knocked over easily by the horse.

In the case of horses which are running at grass the food can be placed in feed troughs, which should be solid enough so that they cannot be turned over easily; where these are made from wood, all exposed edges should be protected by metal strips and the bottoms tinned, otherwise they too will be eaten. Troughs should be sited so that horses will not fall over them in the dark and fifty feet apart so that kicking matches will not develop at feeding time. Unless the animals are quiet and used to being fed together, one trough should be allowed per horse or per mare and foal. Troughs can be bought in the form of a combined hay rack and food trough, in which case all but the most vicious horses will be able to feed from opposite sides of the trough, as they are separated by the hay rack and, when this is full, cannot see each other.

Alternatively hay racks and feed troughs can be placed in a field shelter in the paddock, so that the horses can stand in the dry while they are eating. The shelter should have an almost completely open front so that bullied horses have an easy means of escape. Even so, this method is only suitable for horses which get on well together. As a cheaper alternative, nylon or metal feed troughs (see Fig. 2) may be placed at intervals along a fence, allowing one trough per horse.

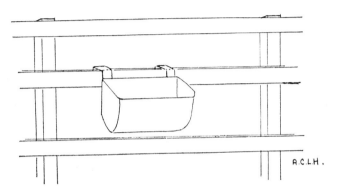

Fig. 2 A metal feed trough placed on the paddock fence

Where very large numbers of horses are to be fed together in a paddock, such as in a riding school or on a stud, it may not be possible to provide troughs for every animal, in which case nuts or cubes should be used rather than oats, as they can be picked up more easily from the ground. At least one extra pile of food than the number of horses should be allowed to prevent fighting; the exact quantity of food will depend on the type of horse being fed and the amount of work it is doing. It is, however, impossible to feed individual rations on this system.

Most horses at grass will rush towards a human who is carrying food and any jealous ones may start to kick and bite their neighbours, which can in turn be very dangerous for the person involved. Therefore most people use a Land Rover or van to distribute nuts or hay among loose horses in a paddock. This is safer than a tractor and trailer, as during a kicking match a horse could easily get pushed over the trailer bar.

Yarded horses should be supplied with hay racks and food troughs constructed along the side walls of the building, again allowing plenty of trough space per horse.

These days, when the cost of feed is so high, it always pays to put some form of manger in loose-boxes or stables to cut the wastage of food to a minimum. If you watch a horse while he is eating, you will probably notice that he tends to push the food out over the sides of the manger. To prevent this, all but the very longest mangers should be provided with metal bars across their corners (see Fig. 3), and the manger should be as deep as possible (at least 1 foot).

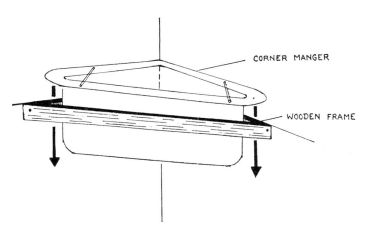

Fig. 3 Corner manger

Preferably, mangers should be blocked in to ground level, to prevent horses from getting cast underneath them (see Fig. 4). They should be made so that they can

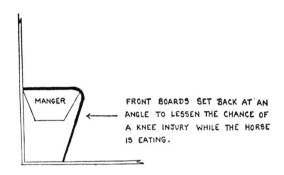

Fig. 4 Long manger fitted with front boards

be lifted out easily for cleaning — this is most important, as nothing will put a horse off his food faster than a dirty manger.

For ease of operation some people prefer to construct a combined manger, hay rack and water trough, all in one, across the back of the stable or loose-box (see Fig. 5). The hay is simply dropped into the compartment on the right and virtually none is wasted, as the horse

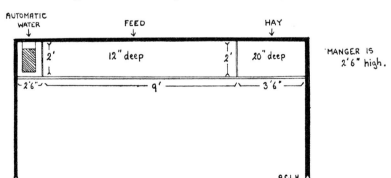

Fig. 5 Combined manger, hay rack and water trough

has to pull it upwards when eating and any seeds and short pieces drop back into the compartment. The water is sited on the opposite side to the hay and the trough should have a drainage plug in the bottom, so that it can be cleaned out easily. An automatic drinking trough ensures that all horses have a constant supply and cannot over-drink at any one time. In a busy stable yard, it also increases the time staff can spend on more productive work. If the long manger is made from wood it will require tinning like the field trough mentioned earlier, otherwise over a period of time the horses will gradually gnaw holes in the bottom. Alternatively, half-glazed drainage tiles can be used and these are much easier to keep clean. This type of manger is particularly good for mares with foals since food can be spread out along its entire length.

Some people prefer to use hay racks. Like hay nets, these should be sited high enough up the wall so that horses cannot get their feet through the bars if they rear up. The main disadvantages of this system are that if they are placed high enough to be safe, they are then too high to fill easily except with a pitchfork, and dust falls down onto the horse.

Hay nets are really only safe for older quiet horses and even then must be kept tied up as high as possible. In order to do this, a second string should be fitted to the bottom of the net and both this string and the original cord which closes the mouth of the net, should be passed in turn through the ring on the stable wall and secured with a slip knot near the bottom of the net. The end of the cord should be passed through the loop of the knot and buried in the net, so that it cannot be undone by the horse. Hay nets should be pulled up tighter periodically during the day and last thing at night, as a long, loose, empty hay net is dangerous.

Automatic water bowls for horses are usually of the

self-filling variety and are available in two distinct patterns: round and oblong as shown below.

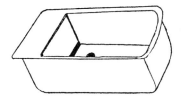

Fig. 6 Automatic water bowl

Great care must be taken to ensure that water bowls are kept clean, especially the area near the automatic filling device which over a period of time tends to get slimy unless it is brushed out regularly. They must also be checked daily to ensure that they are working correctly, as in the event of a blockage a horse might be entirely without water.

Where no automatic water has been laid on, water buckets are used. As there is always the danger that horses will 'play football' with an empty bucket, water buckets should be made from rubber which is almost unbreakable, rather than from plastic. With rough usage metal buckets tend to develop sharp edges which could cut a horse.

Water buckets can be placed in a corner of a loose-box; a round hole which exactly fits the rim of the bucket can be made at one end of a long manger, and the bucket placed in this hole. Alternatively a special bucket holder can be bought but these are safe only as long as there is a bucket in the holder. If a horse pulls the bucket out of its holder, he could then put his leg through the metal bars of the holder with disastrous results.

A constant supply of fresh water must be available to

all horses running at grass; troughs supplied with an auto-matic filling device are the most labour saving — these should have rounded edges and no parts on which a horse could get caught. Field troughs should preferably be fitted with a drainage hole in the bottom, so that they can be cleaned out easily. Automatic water troughs fitted with wheels can be bought; these are connected by means of alkathene tubing to a central water supply and can be wheeled from one paddock to the next, when the horses are moved.

If you are renting a paddock and do not want to go to the expense of installing a water trough for a few horses, then household dustbins can be used but they must be topped up daily and cleaned out regularly. A bucket left in a corner of the paddock would not provide enough water per day for a horse or pony at grass during the summer months.

A river with a shallow bank and a gravel bottom may seem ideal, but these days there is always the risk of pollution.

If ponds are to be used, they must have a shallow bank and should be checked carefully to make sure that no scrap metal, such as bicycles or old buckets, has been thrown into the pond. These could cut a horse badly if he waded into the water. Ponds, rivers and ditches with *steep* banks must be fenced off and an alternative supply of water provided.

2: Basic Food Requirements

Food can be loosely classed as any edible material which is eaten by the horse; not every single part of all food is digestible, so this point must be borne in mind when evaluating a particular type of food.

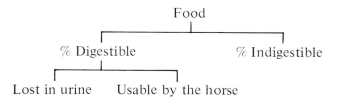

The natural food for horses is plant material or plant products, of which the most common is grass. The horse, as we know him today, therefore depends on plants and grass in particular for his existence (see Fig. 7).

As well as food the horse must have an adequate water supply. Water is normally obtained from two main sources:

1. Drinking water: To a far greater degree than man, horses appear to be able to 'taste' water and always seem to do best on the water they have become used to. Horses should be provided with an *ad lib* supply at all times; under these circumstances they will normally drink only what they require, which is usually in the region of six to eight gallons per day depending on the size of the individual animal, its diet, the work it is doing and weather conditions. Horses brought in hot

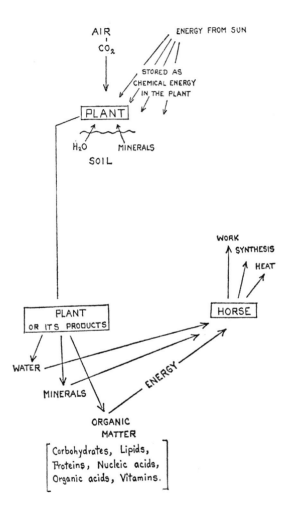

Fig. 7

from work should be offered lukewarm water every ¼ hr, but the quantity, under these circumstances, must be limited to prevent overdrinking. Pregnant mares require slightly more water during the last two to three months of gestation and about one-third more than their normal daily requirement during lactation.

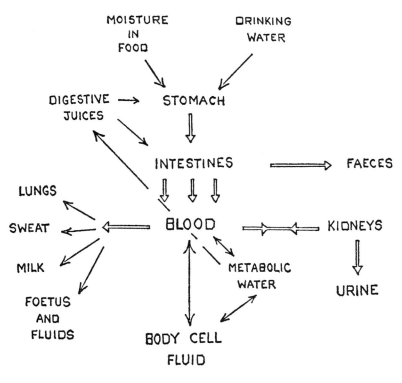

Fig. 8

2. Water present in the food: Foods vary greatly in the amount of water they contain. Concentrates, for example, contain 10—15 per cent moisture, whereas most root

crops can contain 85–90 per cent water. Young leafy grass also has a high water content, which is in the region of 85 per cent. The type of diet fed consequently influences water intake.

Intakes of water and food are closely related – if water is restricted, less food will be eaten; if food is restricted, less water will be drunk. Rather more water is required when animals are on high-protein diets (except perhaps in the case of young spring grass), since more urine is needed to get rid of any excess nitrogen. The more minerals there are in the diet, in particular common salt, the more water the animal will require.

Water is absolutely essential for the maintenance of life and a horse will die sooner if deprived of water than it will if starved of food. When insufficient water is given horses will lose weight rapidly. Therefore automatic watering systems must be checked daily to make sure that they are working normally. When water buckets are used they must be checked several times a day as well as last thing at night to ensure that water is freely available. Most people find that it is both easier and quicker to fill buckets by means of a hosepipe than by hand. Horses will usually drink freely from a bucket while it is being filled by hosepipe, and this eliminates the possibility of staff not refilling buckets properly.

Except for varieties of bean and oil-seed, which contain high levels of protein, fat and oil, most plants are composed mainly of carbohydrate (about 75 per cent) in the form of starch, sugar, and cellulose which is the digestible skeleton and increases as the plant ages.

In their dry matter, unlike plants, animals contain a high percentage of protein but also require high levels of carbohydrate in their diets to provide energy; lack of carbohydrate produces loss of weight and poor condition. Since horses come in all shapes and sizes from

Shires to Shetlands, the energy requirement of any particular horse or pony must be related directly to its size (weight): that is, the bigger the animal, the greater its maintenance energy requirement. However, some authorities maintain that there is a slight increase in the expected requirement as weight increases. Maintenance energy requirements also vary slightly between individuals of the same weight but of differing temperaments. Two other important factors are the amount of work the horse is doing and the temperature of his environment.

Excess energy is stored as fat. Once the horse has finished growing, usually by the time he is three years old, he will tend to put on more fat than he did when he was younger; therefore, the amount of food given to mature horses must be related to the work they are doing. Young horses and those in hard work should have a carbohydrate which is low in fibre. Increased amounts of fibre in a horse's ration lead to a decrease in the digestibility of the other nutrients and to 'pot bellies'.

The fat content of most plants, apart from the oilseeds, is low, but fat provides 2.25 times as much energy as protein and carbohydrate.

Generally the younger the plant the higher its protein content; apart from very young horses and mares in the final stages of gestation and during lactation, the horse does not require high levels of protein in its diet. All living cells contain protein; during digestion the protein in the food is broken down into the amino acids of which it is composed, each protein having its own distinctive pattern of amino acids (see pages 148–52). Plants and some bacteria are capable of synthesising all their own amino acids but animals are unable to do so, so they must already be present in the food if a deficiency is to be avoided. Some amino acids can be produced from others in the liver but several cannot and these are

known as the essential amino acids which are thought
to be:

Arginine	Methionine
Histidine	Phenylalanine
Isoleucine	Threonine
Leucine	Tryptophan
Lysine	Valine

It is known that lysine is an essential amino acid for
the young horse and the other nine may well become
essential under stress conditions.

The term 'essential' can be a little confusing as both
types of amino acid are equally essential to the horse.

A mixture of two or more proteins will often have a
higher feeding value than either one alone, therefore a
considerable variety of different foodstuffs should be
used in a ration.

Under normal circumstances mature horses do not
have a critical requirement for the essential amino acids,
as any deficiency is supplemented by the gut microbes.
Young growing animals, broodmares in the last third of
gestation and during lactation do have a more demanding
pattern, therefore their diets must contain a source of
high-grade protein; also, perhaps, horses in hard work.

As with the energy requirement of horses, the total
quantity of protein needed for maintenance and production varies directly with the weight, use, environment
and age of the individual.

The percentage of protein needed is related to the
animal's appetite, the costiveness of the diet and the
amount of energy it contains.

It is estimated that the following levels of crude
protein expressed as percentages of the total dry matter
in the diet, are required to meet the normal daily needs
of the horse:

Foals — 16 per cent but gradually dropping to 14 per cent by the time the animal is 6 months old.
Yearlings — 12 per cent but gradually dropping to 10 per cent by the time the animal is 18 months old.
Pregnant mares — the maintenance requirement of 8.5 per cent is adequate until the last 90 days of gestation when the requirement increases to 11 per cent.
Lactating mares — the requirement drops gradually from 14 per cent during the first half of lactation to 12 per cent by weaning time.
Mature horses, children's ponies and barren mares — 8.5 per cent.

Protein deficiency will cause depressed appetite, poor growth, loss of weight, reduced milk production, irregular oestrus cycles, lack of stamina, etc.

It is interesting to note that insufficient dietary energy will lead to poor condition but does not affect growth rate.

Vitamins are essential substances, the precursors of which are found in small quantities in raw foods. Plants, including bacteria, are capable of manufacturing their own total vitamin requirements but animals have very limited powers of synthesis and therefore have to rely almost entirely on external supplies. Most substances present in food can only act as vitamins after they have undergone a chemical change. The best known of these is probably β-carotene which is found in carrots, grass and other green crops; it is converted to vitamin A in the walls of the intestine and the liver, excess amounts being stored in the latter organ. In fact, compared to the cow, the horse is said to be capable of retaining four times the quantity of this vitamin in its liver. Carotene is also found in the body fat of horses and cattle. Apart from maize, the carotene content of concentrates normally fed to horses is low. In common with most other vitamins, vitamin A is rapidly destroyed by the effects of exposure to heat and light. Grazing animals obtain more than adequate levels of β-carotene from the grass and build up reserves in their livers, therefore unless a horse has been stabled for a considerable length of time it is very unlikely that it would suffer from a deficiency of this vitamin. Even gestating mares, which have a requirement for vitamin A which is five times greater than other horses, are unlikely to be deficient, but where deficiencies have been produced experimentally, abortions are common.

Vitamin D is found in sun-dried plants and dead leaves; therefore in hay, it is present to a greater or lesser extent depending on the length of time the cut grass has been exposed to the sun. The precursors for this vitamin are found in the skin of both man and animals and the vitamin is formed when the horse is exposed to ultra-violet light; this cannot pass through glass, so the only type of horse which could possibly suffer from a deficiency of vitamin D would be one confined to a stable and not receiving sun-dried hay as part of its diet. Slight deficiencies may occur during periods of dull cloudy weather. Irradiation is known to be more effective in the case of light-skinned horses. Vitamin D is necessary for the normal absorption of calcium and phosphorus from the food.

Vitamin E, or more correctly its precursor α-tocopherol, is found in abundance in young grass and all cereal grains. Therefore horses on a normal diet are unlikely to suffer from any deficiency of this vitamin. Vitamin E (α-tocopherol acetate predominantly) is thought to act as a biological anti-oxidant. A deficiency of the vitamin will cause muscular dystrophy in calves; in horses, vitamin E and selenium help to relieve tying-up. Experiments with rats have shown that a deficiency of the vitamin will cause sterility but this has never been proved conclusively in the case of the horse, although some authorities have noted improvements in breeding performance when a vitamin E supplement was added to the diet; this could be coincidental. Rancidity and also certain foodstuff preservatives are known to destroy vitamin E. For instance, propionic acid-treated grain should be avoided or supplemented with the vitamin.

Vitamin K is necessary for the formation of pro-thrombin which is associated with blood-clotting. It is found in green plants including grass and lucerne.

The B vitamins are generally synthesised by the micro-organisms in the horse's large intestine; there is however some doubt as to whether these organisms are capable of supplying the horse's entire need for these vitamins as their location in the digestive tract leaves little time for total absorption. However, they are widely distributed in the foods which normally make up a horse's diet so, in practice, deficiencies are unlikely to occur except perhaps under stress conditions:

B_1 – found in brewer's yeast, cereal grains, beans, peas and leafy crops. Deficiency symptoms have been reported in horses which have had access to bracken, some samples of which contain a substance which destroys this vitamin.

B_2 – found in all green plants but not to any great extent in cereals.

Nicotinamide – this vitamin is produced by the horse from the amino-acid tryptophan (see page 25), which in turn is present in all cereals.

B_6 – found in yeast, milk and all cereal grains, it plays a part in the absorption of amino acids and dietary energy. In common with other B vitamins it is syn-thesised by the micro-organisms in the gut. A deficiency of this vitamin affects growth rate but is unlikely to occur in horses on a normal diet. Antimetabolites for this vitamin are found in linseed and bracken.

Pantothenic acid — occurs almost everywhere including in all cereal grains.

Folic acid — originally obtained from spinach leaves. Deficiency causes anaemia and poor growth. Prolonged use of any of the sulpha drugs is known to depress the natural bacterial synthesis of this vitamin.

Biotin — present in cereals and vegetables. A deficiency can be caused by feeding significantly large amounts of raw egg — egg white contains a protein-like substance which will combine with biotin to prevent its absorption from the gut.

Choline — is present in green leaves and cereals.

B_{12}— is readily synthesised by micro-organisms and when found in food is directly attributed to them. A deficiency of vitamin B_{12} causes retarded growth. It is the only vitamin known to contain a mineral element — cobalt.

Sulphonamides and antibiotics can affect the availability of the B vitamins by affecting the gut microbes.

Unlike man the horse has a gene in its make-up which enables it to manufacture vitamin C from glucose in its diet. This is principally obtained from the digestion of carbohydrate material, so a supply of this vitamin to horses is unnecessary except perhaps during stress conditions.

Other, unidentified, factors which are said to give positive growth responses, are to be found in such foods as:

Lucerne meal	Dried whey
Fish meal	Dried brewer's grains
Soya bean meal	Residues from alcohol distillation

Under natural conditions horses are unlikely to suffer from the effects of an overdose of vitamins (hypervitaminosis), but when supplements are added to a ration, or more particularly when they are given intravenously, overdosing can occur. Cases of hypervitaminosis in cattle have been reported, mainly in connection with vitamin D which causes abnormally high levels of calcium and phosphorus in the blood, which in turn leads to deposits of calcium salts in the blood vessels.

According to Hintz *et al.* (1973), very high levels of vitamin D in the blood will increase the availability of the phosphorus from bran by approximately one-third, which in turn could precipate a marked calcium deficiency in the diet. Normally only 29.5 per cent of phosphorus in bran is available.

The vitamin requirements of riding horses and in particular thoroughbred racehorses are thought to be higher than the heavy breeds due to the greater stress factors involved.

The minerals present in plants relate directly to the minerals available in the soil in which they were grown. They are usually placed in two groups: the essential elements and the non-essential elements. The former are again divided into major and trace elements and those of significance are listed below:

Major elements:	*Trace elements:*
Calcium	Cobalt
Phosphorus	Iron
Potassium	Zinc
Sodium	Copper
Chlorine	Manganese
Sulphur	Iodine
Magnesium	Molybdenum
	Selenium
	Chromium

These essential elements are the ones which have been proved to have a vital role to play in the horse's metabolism. The trace elements, as their name implies, are present in the animal's body in very small amounts.

Calcium and phosphorus are very important components of the skeleton and as such play a big part in the correct formulation of rations, especially for youngstock and pregnant mares. Horses cannot tolerate a calcium:phosphorus imbalance, particularly if it is the phosphorus which is in excess; for instance 'big head', a condition characterised by lameness and slight enlargement of the lower jaw bones, can be produced by high levels of dietary phosphorus.

Potassium, sodium and chlorine are concerned with the acid-base balance and fluid distribution in the body. Sodium and chlorine are readily available from common salt in the diet or from salt licks, which often also contain the trace element, iodine.

Plants contain very little sodium and chlorine, so a supply of these minerals is essential for horses. The exact requirement depends to a large extent on the following factors: atmospheric temperature and humidity, the work done and the amount of salt already present in the food.

Sulphur is linked to a number of amino acids, e.g. methionine, therefore a sulphur deficiency could occur only where there was a protein deficiency in the diet.

Bran and most vegetable proteins are good sources of magnesium, its main role in the body being that of an enzyme activator.

Mineral supplementation of diets must always be carried out with care, as it is most important that an accurate balance is maintained between the various elements otherwise metabolic disorders can result. For example the calcium:phosphorus ratio should be maintained within the range of 1.1:1 to 2:1. Most plant material is high in phosphorus, so a calcium supplement should be fed to adjust this, particularly in the case of youngstock and broodmares, otherwise epiphysitis and bone conditions such as osteomalacia can result. The horse is also affected by toxic levels of some of the trace elements, such as: copper, selenium, molybdenum and chromium; copper in particular is a cumulative poison. Great care should therefore be taken when giving supplements in the feed. If more than one supplement is used at the same time, e.g. when an already supplemented cube feed is given and another additive is used at the same time, overdoses of certain elements could result, which over a period of time might lead to the death of the horse.

Older horses, that is those in their late teens and onwards, are generally thought to have a reduced ability to absorb calcium and phosphorus from their diet, therefore older breeding stock in particular should have their diets carefully supplemented with vitamins and minerals. However, some authorities have noted that very young broodmares are more sensitive to vitamin deficiencies than older mares.

Last but by no means least, horses and ponies need to be kept reasonably warm; no amount of food will maintain the horse in good condition if it is kept in a cold, draughty stable. Using food to maintain body warmth is a very expensive practice these days. Horses can be kept more economically in warm but well-ventilated boxes in cold weather.

3: Digestion

Most foods have to be broken down into simpler substances before they can pass through the lining of the gut and enter the blood and lymphatic systems. This breakdown is known as digestion.

The process of digestion in the horse can be subdivided into the following processes:

1. Mechanical:

   the act of chewing and the muscular contractions in the alimentary tract, which cause the food to be moved along the gut;

2. Chemical action:

   principally the action of the various enzymes present in the digestive juices;

3. Microbial digestion:

   this occurs mainly in the large intestine.

In order that the various enzymes can act efficiently, the food has to be broken up into smaller pieces before it is swallowed.

The horse has six incisors in both its upper and lower jaws (see Fig. 9). These are used for cutting the food, in particular grass, which is then drawn into the mouth by the tongue and passed back to the molars where it is ground. The molar teeth, of which there are twelve in both the upper and the lower jaws, are ridged along their surface to assist the grinding process. However, with wear they tend to form sharp edges and if these are not filed down regularly, they dig into the side of the tongue or the cheeks, causing what are known as buccal ulcers to form (see Fig. 10). These are very painful and

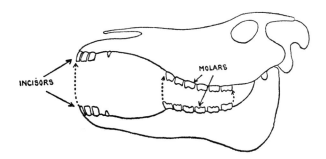

Fig. 9 Skull showing position of incisors and molars

will cause an affected horse to drop partly chewed food out of its mouth, known as 'quidding'. They also reduce the efficiency of the chewing process which in turn affects digestion and with it the condition of the animal. With time, the molars tend to wear smooth, so very old horses may need to be fed on mashes and other soft foods if their condition is to be maintained.

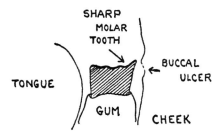

Fig. 10 Diagram showing how a sharp tooth can cause buccal ulcers

Another factor which can adversely affect the horse's ability to graze efficiently, is a condition known as 'parrot mouth' (Figs. 11a and b). In this case the incisors overlap and the bottom teeth close on the roof of the mouth just behind the base of the top teeth, which means that the affected horse has to tear the grass off and is virtually unable to graze short herbage.

Horses and ponies should have their teeth checked once a year to make quite certain that all is well, particularly if they are parrot-mouthed or have had a tooth removed for any reason. The older the horse becomes

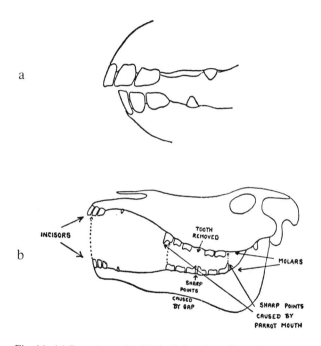

Fig. 11 (a) Parrot mouth; (b) skull showing effect of parrot mouth on molars

the more important this annual check is; however, younger horses with apparently normal mouths should not be neglected, as they too can have problems with their teeth.

The digestive tract is composed of the mouth, gullet,

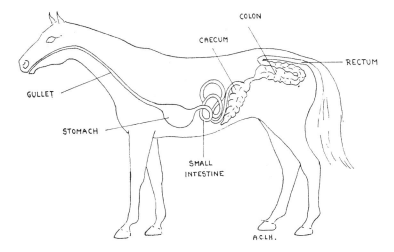

Fig. 12 The digestive system

stomach, small intestine, caecum, colon and rectum
(Fig. 12). Its function is to take in food, grind it up,
swallow, digest, absorb the nutrients and eliminate any
waste matter. The horse does not ruminate.

The presence of food in the mouth activates the
production of saliva and this aids swallowing. The food
passes down the gullet into the stomach, which in the
thoroughbred mare has a capacity of only 8.4 litres, as
compared with 39–84 litres in cattle. The food passes
through the stomach and indeed as far as the colon at a
rate estimated to be three times faster than the rate in
cattle (Linerode, 1966). Because of the way in which
the stomach is made, the horse is virtually unable to be
sick – a procedure which greatly helps other species at
times. In the natural state the horse has to rely on its
speed for survival. It has a relatively large lung capacity
for its size and this coupled with the small stomach
area helps to make it an efficient galloping machine.

Due to its small size in comparison to that of the cow and the rate at which the food passes through it, only partial digestion and fermentation can occur in the stomach, but the presence of food stimulates the production of large quantities of stomach juices, which help to regulate the pyloric stomach contents to a pH of 2.5, which in turn ensures that any fermentation yields principally lactic acid, which is a valuable source of energy for the horse. The presence of food in the stomach also stimulates the production of pancreatic juice which is necessary for intestinal function.

Unlike other farm animals the horse does not have a gall bladder but does produce bile in the liver, which flows into the small intestine, where fat consumed in the ration is digested and absorbed. The horse can tolerate relatively large amounts of fat in its diet. In an experiment ponies were fed a ration containing 20 per cent corn oil, without any ill effects.

The small intestine is approximately four times the size of the stomach. Nearly all the digestion which takes place in the small intestine is due to the action of the enzymes; basically these convert starch into glucose, which is absorbed through the gut wall. Likewise a proportion of the protein is broken down into its constituent amino acids and absorbed through the gut wall.

The normal diet of horses in the United Kingdom is composed mainly of hay, oats and bran, as well as grass; as all these contain cellulose, the breakdown of cellulose to produce energy is one of the most important aspects of equine digestion. Unlike ruminants, this occurs in the large intestine after digestion by enzymes. Any enzyme action in the large intestine is due to a carry-over from the small intestine and enzymes produced by the micro-organisms which inhabit the large intestine, as the glands in the large intestine are thought only to

produce mucus. These organisms require a source of
nitrogen in order to survive and build up microbial
protein. This is normally supplied by the natural inter-
change of urea through the gut wall, which is produced

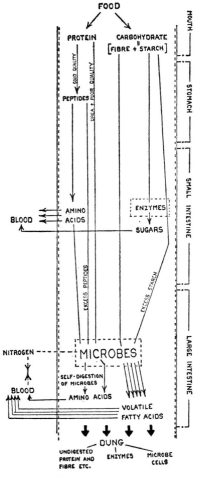

Fig. 13 Digestion of protein and carbohydrate in the mature horse

as a result of 'non-essential amino-acid production in the liver, together with any urea which may have been included in the ration and excess protein.

The fact that not all the protein is broken down and

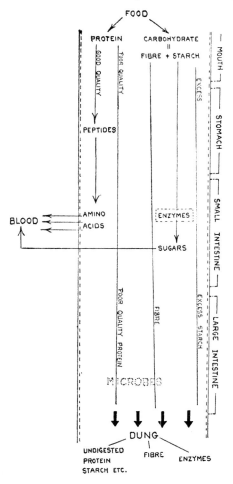

Fig. 14 Digestion of protein and carbohydrate in the young horse or pony

digested in the small intestine is probably due to the rate of passage through this organ, also some protein may have been trapped and sheltered by the cellulose and lignin fraction of the diet and this will pass undigested into the large intestine and so add to the available supply of nitrogen. In addition there is the protein supplied when the microbial cells themselves are broken down by self-digestion, the amino acids they have built up are released and a proportion absorbed through the gut wall (Slade *et al.*, 1971). This microbial protein is of good quality and highly digestible; therefore, assuming that a high percentage is probably absorbed, the adult horse or pony which has developed a full complement of intestinal micro-organisms will not suffer from an amino-acid deficiency and so does not need a diet containing only high-quality proteins (unless it is a broodmare in the final stages of gestation, during lactation or a horse in hard work), and always providing that the diet contains adequate amounts of carbohydrate and digestible roughage. In theory then, most essential amino-acid deficiencies in the adult will be made good in sufficient quantities by the breakdown and absorption of microbial protein from the large intestine.

One of the basic principles of feeding horses is to avoid making sudden changes in the diet; this is because the species and number of each species of microbe which inhabit the horse's gut vary with the type of food the horse is receiving at any particular time and this affects digestion. Any change in diet should therefore be made gradually, so that the necessary change in species or number of each species of microbe is complete before the horse is finally put on to his new diet. When antibiotics are added to the food, they can have a detrimental effect on the normal micro-organisms as well as any pathogenic ones and cause a digestive diarrhoea.

The gut microbes obtain their supply of energy by

breaking down cellulose and utilising any starch and lactic acid which enters the large intestine and using some of the energy produced for their own needs, the remainder being absorbed through the gut wall as volatile fatty acids and so utilised by the horse. The end product of the microbial fermentation of cellulose is mainly acetic acid and this is not used as efficiently as glucose in the horse's metabolism, glucose being the end product of starch digestion in the small intestine. Since glucose is considered to be the better source of energy for muscle metabolism, horses kept for their athletic ability, such as racehorses and eventers, should receive diets low in fibre (hay) and high in starch (grain). This can be achieved, for instance, by feeding clipped oats instead of unclipped, reducing the quantity of hay and increasing the grain. This type of diet produces less bulk in the large intestine which is an added advantage when athletic ability is important.

Vitamins of the B complex are produced in the large intestine and absorbed.

Waste material is voided through the anus and consists mainly of water, undigested material including lignin, cells from the lining of the gut, excess minerals, bacteria and products of bacterial decomposition, together with various digestive secretions. The various parts of the digestive tract are thought to have their own optimum pH range at which digestion is most efficient; marked changes in this range would indicate errors in diet which would affect the health of the animal. In the horse, a pH range for faeces of between 6.2 and 6.3 is considered normal and a pH range of 6.9 to 7.6 is associated with certain abnormalities e.g. eczema (Mansson, 1957).

The rate at which food travels along the digestive tract governs its digestibility and degree of assimilation. It has been estimated that most of the food (a normal hay and oat ration) will pass through the stomach and small intestine in under twelve hours; half the waste material will have been voided by thirty-six hours and 75 per cent by about seventy-two hours.

It therefore follows that the larger the quantity of food passing through these areas at any one time, the lower the degree of actual assimilation; so it is better to feed horses 'little and often'. Digestion is improved by light exercise but is impaired by heavy, fast work, therefore horses should never be worked immediately after a large feed.

At birth foals have no microbes in their large intestine; these develop gradually during the first seven months of life, and until they are present in large numbers the foal is incapable of digesting significant amounts of fibre. Most of the digestion in the young horse or pony, therefore, takes place in the stomach and small intestine and no fibre is broken down at all initially. The lack of significant numbers of micro-organisms in the foal's large intestine is thought to be one cause of early scours which sometimes occur about the time they first start to eat hay.

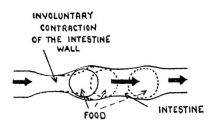

Fig. 15 Peristalsis

Food is transported along the length of the gut by means of waves of involuntary muscular contractions in the gut walls (Fig. 15).

Anything which interferes with these contractions

also interferes with digestion, causing colic pains and/or a twisted gut. These waves can be heard quite plainly if one listens to the horse's flank; they are known as peristalsis and the sound which is heard is known as borborygmi. It is the sound that the veterinary surgeon listens for when examining a horse with suspected colic.

Intestinal parasites also interfere with the maximum absorption of nutrients and can on occasion cause colic due to blockages, pressure on the mesenteric nerve ganglia or reduced function of parts of the gut. Adult horses usually develop an immunity to the effects of these parasites but they can be fatal in foals and yearlings.

4: Dried Grass, Hay and Silage

Dried grass

Dried grass, which is probably the most underrated food for horses and ponies at the present time, is made by passing a current of hot air over freshly cut or field-wilted herbage. The exact temperature depends on the type of machine used, but the main idea is to reduce the material from 80 per cent moisture down to 10 per cent moisture without appreciably altering its nutritive value (heat treatment partly de-natures protein but this increases its value). The dried herbage can then be passed through a hammer mill which reduces it to a meal; it is either marketed in this form or cubed, using molasses or steam as the binding material, otherwise it is sold in a loose, chopped form, or compressed into cobs or wafers. The nutritional value of the finished product is very similar to that of the fresh crop and as such provides a very valuable addition to the winter diet of most horses. Like good hay, it should be green and not brown with a caramel smell which would denote over-heating during drying. Dried grass is mostly available immediately after harvesting, i.e. during the summer period, but it will keep well right through the winter.

A list of producers throughout the United Kingdom and Republic of Ireland can be obtained from:

> The British Association of Green Crop Driers Ltd,
> 16 Lonsdale Gardens,
> Tunbridge Wells,
> Kent TN1 1PD.

Dried grass is normally available in every area of the British Isles and dried lucerne is available in the areas where it is normally grown, i.e. mainly in the eastern counties.

Horse owners should look on dried grass (or lucerne) as a valuable replacement for bran in the diet, as, unlike bran, it does not interfere with the calcium:phosphorus ratio of the ration.

Dried green crops are sometimes marketed under a star rating system which accounts for both the percentage crude protein and percentage fibre; the latter gives an indication of the energy value of the product. The protein values normally lie between 14 and 20 per cent on a fresh weight basis.

Under the Fertilizer and Feeding Stuffs Regulations,

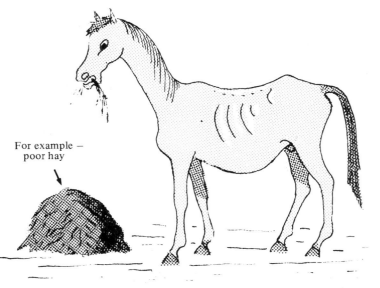

For example – poor hay

A horse may receive the correct amount of food but still be under-fed if the energy value of the food is too low for his needs.

the term 'dried green roughage' is used for material with a protein level of less than 12 per cent. Low-protein wafers can also be obtained from some producers and these make a good chop substitute when soaked to break them down and then mixed into the normal ration.

Since grass meal is low in sodium, a salt lick must be provided.

Both grass and lucerne meals appear to be very palatable and are accepted with relish by most horses, but they should be introduced into the ration gradually and not offered at the full rate until the horses are used to the new taste.

The easiest way to feed grass meal is to put some water into the bottom of a bucket and add the meal, then stir it round until it has absorbed all the water. Only sufficient water should be used to wet the meal, unless you intend to feed a mash. The damp meal is then added to the rest of the feed. Many horses will eat grass or lucerne nuts but some individuals will reject them, in which case they can be broken down into a meal by soaking overnight in a little water.

Legumes, including lucerne, due to their high protein content, tend to cause horses to stale slightly more than usual (their droppings are also looser); this is just Nature's way of getting rid of surplus nitrogen. Therefore, horses on high protein diets must have access to an *ad lib* supply of water.

Hay

This is the most popular method of conserving grass; the younger it is cut the higher the moisture content and the more difficult it is to dry, therefore 'in the old days' people tended to leave the crop until it had become more mature and the moisture content was consequently lower. However, these days modern haymaking machinery allows us to cut the crop at an earlier stage and dry it rapidly with little risk of spoilage.

The earlier the grass is cut the higher is its nutritive value, and the longer it is left uncut the higher is the lignin and fibre content and the lower the nutritive value. As far as horses are concerned a very clean hay is essential, therefore many horse owners tend to buy a more mature type of rye-grass hay which traditionally is usually the cleanest but not the best from a nutritional point of view.

The main idea in hay making is to reduce the moisture content of the grass from 80 per cent in the standing crop, down to 15 to 20 per cent in the bale, which in turn will inhibit the action of the plant enzymes which cause heating and mould growth etc. The faster the crop is dried the less likely any loss of nutrients. If drying is slow, some of the sugars are converted to carbon dioxide and water by plant enzymes, giving a higher lignin and cellulose content.

Long drying in the field may increase the vitamin D content but as the hay is bleached so the pro-vitamin A (carotene) is lost.

Rain has the greatest effect on a crop once it has been turned and therefore partially dried. It prolongs the action of the plant enzymes and causes mould growth – therefore, as far as possible, hay which has been rained on should not be bought for feeding to horses.

Lucerne hay is particularly rich in protein and calcium, while clover hay is nearly as good. Lucerne hay is used extensively for horses in many parts of the world, but both lucerne and clover need more drying than grass hay, so are not so readily available in the British Isles.

Timothy and cocksfoot hays have the lowest digestible crude-protein values, with ryegrass and meadow fescue a close second; a good mixture of various grasses and clover gives a better value. Care must be taken to ensure that the hay has come from 'clean' land. Most animals will avoid poisonous weeds when grazing but will often eat them when they are included in the hay. Hay made from the long grass rejected by horses in their paddocks during spring and summer should not be used for horses as it may well contain droppings and worm larvae.

These days it really pays most horse owners to grow their own hay or buy it off the field at hay-time. Even though there is, on average, a 15 per cent loss in weight between harvest and Christmas, this still works out cheaper in most years. A Dutch barn or some similar building is essential for hay storage.

Few changes occur in the stack if the hay is baled at less than 15 per cent moisture, but a higher nutritive value is obtained by baling earlier at higher moisture levels to retain more leaf and then using an in-barn hay drier to reduce the moisture content as quickly as possible.

The barn floor, which must be well drained and dry, should be covered with wooden slats placed over some loose straw to reduce wastage of the bottom bales to a minimum and these bales should be stacked on their cut sides for the same reasons. The bales should then be stacked round the drier funnel, leaving no gaps which would allow the hot air to escape. (See also Barn hay drying in Glossary.)

At high moisture levels in the stack, oxidation of the sugars occurs and hexoses tend to combine with the amino acids to produce a brown (mowburnt) hay. Thermophilic bacteria (those which live in high temperatures) can go on acting up to just over 70°C, and above this temperature oxidation can cause further heat which tends to accumulate and eventually produce combustion. Even at slightly increased temperatures there is a lowering of the nutritive value, therefore bales must be dried as quickly as possible.

Moulds tend to grow on the outside bales of a stack. Therefore, when buying hay from a stack any mouldy bales should be discarded. Some moulds produce toxins which are carcinogenic, while the spores can cause broken wind, abortions and guttural pouch mycosis.

The following points should be borne in mind when examining hay to determine its possible nutritive value:

(i) The colour: the more green it is the higher is the pro-vitamin A content;

(ii) Smell: there must be no trace of mould, the hay should smell sweet but not mowburnt;

(iii)Touch: the higher the lignin content, the more prickly the sample will feel and the lower its digestibility. A good sample should feel smooth, pliable and dry; damp samples usually feel soft.

Grasses cut at an early stage produce a high protein/low fibre hay, and those cut when they are mature produce a low protein/high fibre hay; therefore, the amount of leaf to stalk in the sample is important as the leaf contains 80 per cent of the nutrients.

Hay bellies are produced by the horse or pony having to eat large quantities of poor-quality hay, which is mainly digested in the large intestine and so accumulates there causing distension of this organ. Hay bellies can be reduced by feeding at least some of the hay in the form of chop, as this causes less distension of the caecum.

Chop is made by passing long hay through a chop cutter, which consists of knives rotated either by means of a handle or powered by a tractor. Chop helps to prevent greedy horses from bolting their food, but since the horse has a limited capacity for food, chop really only has a place in the diet of adult horses doing slow work or out of work altogether. Hay and/or chop alone will provide this type of horse with at least 90 per cent of the nutrients he requires, but a salt lick and *ad lib* water must also be supplied.

The safest method of feeding hay is to put it in a pile
in a corner of the loose-box but the current high value
of this food prompts most people to put their hay into
hay racks or nets, rather than let the horse use some of
it for bedding. Hay racks do tend to allow hay seeds to
drop into the horse's eyes and they are usually too high
up the wall for young foals to be able to reach them.
These racks can also be dangerous playthings for young
horses, as should they rear up at a hay rack with bars
down the front, a front hoof could slip between the bars
and cause a serious accident. Likewise horses and ponies
can get tied up in hay nets. To minimise the risk of an
accident and so make the net slightly more safe, two
strings should be attached — one acting as the normal

STRING TIED
TO ITSELF

DANGEROUS

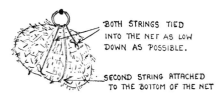

BOTH STRINGS TIED
INTO THE NET AS LOW
DOWN AS POSSIBLE.

SECOND STRING ATTACHED
TO THE BOTTOM OF THE NET

LESS DANGEROUS

Fig. 16 Correct and incorrect method of securing a hay net

draw string and the other tied to the bottom of the net; both strings are then passed through the ring and tied as far down the net as possible, forcing the net as high up the wall as it will go (Fig. 16). It is also particularly important to make sure that hay nets in horse boxes and trailers are as far out of the way of the horse's front feet as possible during a journey. Probably the safest method of saving hay is to construct a container in the corner of the loose-box or stable according to the diagram on page 16.

Silage

Silage is thought of by most people in terms of a cattle feed, but work done at the Irish National Stud has proved beyond doubt that it can be used for barren mares and other adult horses not in work.

Silage is the term used to describe the material produced by the anaerobic fermentation of fresh grass or other crops. Ensilage is the term used to describe the process.

However a word of warning: early in 1984 several horses died or became ill after being fed 'big bale' silage. The cause was found to be a toxin-producing organism from the same family as the tetanus bacillus – Clostridium botulinum type B. Like the tetanus bacillus this organism is found in soil. The low pH of clamp silage tends to destroy any pathogens which may be present. Big bale silage on the other hand has a relatively high pH – the drier the silage the higher the pH and this allows these organisms to remain viable.

Another possible danger associated with 'big bale' silage is that due to the size of the bales, moulds may develop in opened bales before the whole bale can be used. Moulds in both hay and silage are known to be dangerous (see page 49).

It is therefore recommended that 'big bale' silage is not fed to horses unless extensive tests have first been carried out to determine its safety.

The horses that died or were destroyed showed signs of progressive paralysis.

Haylage or Horsehage

These are just the trade names for material which has been wilted down to high dry matter levels, precision chopped and processed through a Harvestore tower silo. The product is stored and sold in polythene bags. Since rats and mice are attracted by black polythene steps should be taken to keep the buildings rodent free. Even a 1 cm. diameter hole can spoil the contents of a whole bag. Haylage and Horsehage are sold especially for feeding to horses.

5: Cereal Grains

Cereal grains are composed mainly of carbohydrate which is in the form of starch and often represent the main source of energy for the horse.

Oats are the traditional feed for horses and no other grain can quite take their place for this purpose, but as they are lacking in some of the essential amino acids they need supplementing to form a truly balanced food. Maize and barley are also used to a limited extent in the United Kingdom.

Wheat, as such, due to its high gluten content, is not considered a suitable feed for horses, but bran, which is the seed coat, is used extensively in some stables, especially for making mashes.

The crude protein content of grain varies little between oats, flaked maize and barley, all being in the region of 11 per cent, but their value for promoting growth is linked more closely with the amino-acid composition of the individual grain. All grain samples are deficient in lysine and methionine, with little to choose between oats and barley, and maize being the most deficient.

Oats and maize contain almost twice as much oil as barley, the oil content of oats being in the region of 5 per cent. The oil is unsaturated and rapidly becomes rancid when the grain is crushed and/or if the moisture content is above 16 per cent. Therefore, grain should normally never be put into store at more than 16 per cent moisture, preferably less; after crushing, it should not be kept for more than two to four weeks, depending on the weather. A high percentage of water leads to heating in store, which in turn leads to mite-infestation and deterioration. If the grain becomes rancid vitamin E is also destroyed.

All cereal grains are deficient in calcium and have a calcium:phosphorus ratio of approximately 1:3; a percentage of the phosphorus is in the form of phytates. Some phytate phosphorus is made available in the stomach by plant phytate enzymes and some may be hydrolysed by bacterial phytases in the large intestine, but utilisation of phytates by horses is probably less efficient than in ruminants. According to Hintz *et al.* (1973), only 29.5 per cent of the phosphorus is available to the horse under normal dietary conditions, so this still leaves an incorrectly balanced calcium:phosphorus ratio, which should not be less than 1.1 : 1, even for adult horses. Added to this, oat phytases in particular are capable of immobilising calcium in the diet. There-fore, horses and ponies should always receive a calcium supplement to their grain ration.

Cereal grains are deficient in vitamin D and apart from maize are also deficient in pro-vitamin A.

Oats

The food value of oats depends on the percentage of husk to kernel, the average being just under 30 per cent, and varies with the variety and the weather conditions during growth and harvest.

The energy needs of horses vary with each individual, its age, size and the type of work it is doing. An increase in dietary energy is best provided by increasing the grain and decreasing the fibre. Therefore oat samples should be selected carefully for animals with a high energy requirement. A high-quality (high starch/low fibre) sample will appear shiny and round, with the kernel almost bursting out of its husk; poor samples, those with a high fibre content, are long and thin in appearance and the husk often looks dull.

To reduce the fibre content still further, oats are usually clipped before feeding to horses – this can be done in several different ways: by passing the grain down a conveyor fitted with a paddle blade to remove the top of the husk which is then dropped through a mesh at the end of the machine; or by passing the grain along a conveyor system which purely by means of friction removes the ends of the husk. A more sophisticated method, based on the same principles, consists of first sieving off any foreign matter or soil and then passing the grain down a rotating shaft fitted with beaters or brushes, according to whether the grain is to be clipped or polished. The husk and dust are usually blown clear into a collection hopper. A similar process is used to remove the awns from barley grains.

Oats must be cleaned and re-cleaned before use to remove any foreign materials, weed seeds, etc. New grain should be stored until Christmas to prevent digestive upsets.

The husk tends to form a barrier to the digestive juices so that, unless they are well chewed first, whole grains will usually pass straight through the stomach and small intestine and are only made available by microbial digestion in the large intestine; therefore most people either bruise or crush oats before feeding, to reduce wastage. This is done by passing the whole grain through rollers which can be adjusted from barely cracking the grain to rolling it completely flat. Many horse owners prefer to feed their grain bruised rather than crushed, as the more heavily the grain is crushed the more dust is created (see Chapter 11).

Oats available in the United Kingdom are grown mainly in England and Scotland, the Scottish variety generally being considered superior to its English

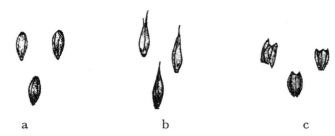

Fig. 17 (a) Clipped oats; (b) unclipped oats; (c) crushed clipped oats

counterpart. In some seasons, however, there is little to choose between them. In dry summers, Scotland tends to score due to the damper climate. At one time oats were all stacked and threshed, but now most farmers north of the border also combine their oats, so this factor has virtually been eliminated. Damper climates tend to produce a thinner-skinned grain. Good samples are sometimes shipped from Australia and Canada but these cost about half as much again as home-grown oats and are therefore uneconomical in most seasons.

Barley

Barley is used extensively in the rations of farm animals other than horses; it has a much higher energy value than oats, and a lower fibre content, so represents a considerably more fattening and heating food than

Fig. 18 (a) Whole barley; (b) boiled whole barley

oats. Therefore, if used for horses, barley should be given only in moderation.

Horses are mostly kept for their athletic ability, so over-fatness is detrimental. However, barley does have a place as an aid to the fattening of thin horses, or the preparation of animals for the show-ring and sales, where above-average levels of body fat are usually considered desirable.

Show horses and yearlings being prepared for sale are often given whole barley which is boiled together with linseed and fed as a mash. Like oats, barley should be stored before feeding.

Micronised and steam rolled barley may be bought and as they are cooked are safer to feed than raw barley which may be fed rolled, in a dry feed, but only small quantities should be given at a time. Barley with a moisture content of about 17 per cent should be used for rolling, so unless the grain has been previously treated with the preservative propionic acid (propcorn), moulds will develop and the keeping quality is poor. However, when using propionic acid treated grain a vitamin E supplement should be given.

Some by-products of the brewing industry are sometimes fed to horses. During brewing the barley is soaked and allowed to germinate for about six days; during this period enzymes develop which are capable of hydrolysing starch to sugars. The grain is dried and the sprouts are removed and sold as malt culms. Malt culms contain about 24 per cent crude protein and are relatively high in fibre but low in starch; they can be used for horses but need soaking first, otherwise they will swell in the stomach and cause colic.

The dried grains are crushed, water is added and the mixture heated to about 64°C. The enzymes then convert the starch to sugars and the sugary liquid is drawn off leaving the brewer's grains. These are sold either wet or dried and can be fed in moderation to horses in either form. Wet brewer's grains stay fresh for only a matter of days rather than weeks, unless they are ensiled.

The sugary liquid is boiled up with hops, the hops are filtered out and the liquid allowed to ferment, producing alcohol and carbon dioxide. The yeast is finally filtered out, dried and sold as dried brewer's yeast, which contains about 42 per cent protein; it is also a valuable source of the B vitamins, except B_{12}.

Maize (Indian corn)

The normal yellow maize or Indian corn contains a precursor of vitamin A known as cryptoxanthin. Maize is a high-energy food, containing about 84 per cent starch, but is low in proteins and those present are of a poor quality. It is also low in fibre and contains almost no calcium. Plant breeders have succeeded, however, in producing certain varieties of maize with improved levels of lysine and methionine. Maize also contains about 4.5 per cent oil, which is mostly in the form of unsaturated fatty acids.

Flaked maize is obtained by passing moistened grain through steam heated rollers. Alternatively it may be micronised using infra-red heat, then rolled. This is very palatable and of slightly improved digestibility as compared with the uncooked grain.

Maize germ meal is sometimes used for horses. This is produced by soaking the ground grain. The germ then floats to the surface and is skimmed off. Some of the oil is extracted before the meal is produced, but the final product can contain up to 14 per cent oil, up to 14.6 per cent crude protein and up to 84 per cent starch.

Bran

Wheat as such should never be fed to horses; the grain consists of about 85 per cent endosperm (the part used for flour), 2 per cent germ (mostly sold for human consumption), and 13 per cent bran or seed coat.

When milling wheat, the main object is to separate the endosperm from its seed coat, with as little flour wasted as possible. The grain is passed through a series of rollers arranged in pairs, which tear off the coat (bran) and just leave the endosperm, which is then crushed to form flour.

Bran is usually sold in three grades: giant; broad and fine; or a mixture of all three which is known as straight-run bran. There is little difference in nutritive value between the grades; the main difference lies in its ability to keep the ration open. The larger the flakes the better, as these are also less dusty.

Bran is high in fibre, containing about 12 per cent crude fibre, about 17 per cent crude protein and a low starch energy value, it is also very low in calcium and high in phosphorus.

When fed dry, bran will help to counteract a digestive diarrhoea and when used as a mash it has well-known laxative properties (see Chapter 13).

Middlings or thirds are really too fine and dusty to be an ideal feed for horses but they have a higher energy value than bran.

Other grains

Rye is not very palatable and can cause digestive upsets, so is seldom if ever used for animal feeding.

Rough rice is used as horse feed in some parts of the world. Millet is also used in the tropics and warm temperate regions; it has a nutritive value similar to that of oats. Sorghum is similar to, but smaller than, maize, and is used in parts of the southern states of America, in India and in Africa.

Other high-energy feeds

On arrival at the factory sugar beet is washed, sliced and soaked in water to remove the sugar. After extraction the pulp is dried to 10 per cent moisture. The residue has 18 per cent crude fibre and 9 per cent crude protein. Frequently molasses is added to the beet pulp, which is sold as 'dried molassed beet pulp', either shredded or cubed. Cubed pulp must be soaked for 24 hours before feeding to horses, and shredded pulp overnight. Soak the pulp in 1½ times its own weight of water.

Beet molasses is a highly palatable, laxative food containing about 65 per cent sugar. It is used extensively as a binding agent in the manufacture of compound cubes.

6: Protein Foods

In practice stabled horses are fed on cereal (i.e. principally oats) based diets. Therefore the protein foods used must be chosen for their ability to correct the amino-acid deficiencies of the cereals. The principal amino-acid deficiencies in all cereals are lysine and methionine, so these should be taken as a measure of the quality of any protein for horse rations (see tables on pages 149-152).

The nutritional value of protein is usually expressed in terms of 'digestible crude protein', but the digestibility can be affected by such factors as processing and level of feeding. Also it does not take into account the amino-acid composition, which is probably a better criterion for horse rations.

The following are the most common protein concentrates fed to horses in home-mixed rations:

Linseed   Dried skim milk powder
Extracted soya bean meal   Raw eggs
Full fat soya bean meal   Dried grass meal (high
Field beans   protein grades)

Others are incorporated into nuts, most of which are not sufficiently palatable to feed in the straight form; these include:

Groundnut meal   Locust beans
Cottonseed meal   Fish meal
Palm kernel meal   Dried brewer's yeast
Coconut meal
Sunflower meal
Sesame meal

The six meals in the left-hand column are what is left after most of the oil has been removed from the oil-seeds: they are rich in protein and form an important and valuable supplement to grain rations.

The seeds are first broken up, crushed and then cooked; the oil is removed by means of a screw press or by using a chemical solvent, in which case the residue is sometimes toasted to improve the sample and hasten evaporation of the solvent. Some seeds have a hard outer husk and this has to be removed to increase the digestibility of the sample; the process is known as decorticating, and consists of simply cracking and riddling the residue.

Most of the protein present in oil-seeds is in the form of true protein. It is highly digestible and of good quality (see amino-acid composition of foods on page 150), but not quite the quality of animal protein such as fish meal, milk and eggs. Oil-seed protein is usually deficient in one or more of the essential amino acids, including lysine, therefore most of the oil-seeds, except soya beans, cannot fully supplement a grain ration without the additional aid of animal protein.

The energy value of the oil-seeds is greatly enhanced by the amount of oil which is left after processing; however, too much oil can lead to digestive disturbances.

Oil-seeds are generally high in phosphorus and low in calcium, so supplementation with calcium is necessary.

Linseed

These are seeds from a plant of the flax family *linum usitatissimum.* They contain up to 10 per cent mucilage, which can only be digested by the microbes in the large intestine. The mucilage is readily dispersed in water to form a jelly-like substance. Linseed contains 39 per cent oil and 26 per cent crude protein, the amino-acid composition of which can be seen on page 151. The calcium:phosphorus ratio is 1:2, therefore, as with all other oil-seeds, a calcium supplement must be given to balance the diet.

Most, if not all, samples of linseed contain the cyanogenic glycoside, linamarin and its associated enzyme, linase, which together under warm, damp conditions will produce the poison, hydrogen cyanide. The enzyme is, however, destroyed by boiling, so to be on the safe side all linseed fed to horses should be boiled before feeding. Simply pouring boiling water over the linseed or a mix containing linseed, would not produce sufficient heat to destroy the enzyme.

Linseed meals are usually heated during processing which kills all the linase and most of the linamarin, so they are normally quite safe to feed.

Linseed is primarily used as an important constituent of mashes for horses and ponies, its primary claim to fame being its ability to improve the general coat condition and shine (see Chapter 13).

Good samples of linseed should appear clean and shiny, and the grain should be plump rather than flat.

Fig. 19 Linseed

Extracted and full-fat soya bean meal

Soya beans are mainly imported from America, but some also come from Canada and France. The beans themselves are round and cream coloured, they contain up to 21 per cent oil but this may be solvent extracted and the meal which is left contains only about 1 per cent oil. It is the best source of vegetable protein available for animal feeding, as of all the oil-seeds it approximates most closely to animal protein; it is therefore a valuable addition to the normal grain ration.

Full fat soya bean meal contains 18 per cent oil and 37 per cent protein. It is steam heated to destroy any anti-nutritional factors and is extruded to maximise the availability of the oil. The meal is an attractive golden colour, slightly granular in texture with a pleasant biscuit aroma.

It should not be stored for longer than one month in cold weather or two weeks in warm weather, otherwise the oil may become rancid.

The amount of soya bean meal included in a ration should not exceed 15 per cent.

Toasted or steam heated meal is used for horses as this destroys a trypsin inhibitor which the raw beans contain, which in turn reduces peptide (amino acid) digestion. The heating process is carefully controlled as overheating will also destroy lysine and arginine.

Animals must be introduced to soya bean meal gradually with only very small amounts given at first. Full fat soya can be included in the rations of show horses, to improve coat condition, also the energy and protein value of the ration.

Field beans

Otherwise known as Horse beans, these are grown over a wide area of the British Isles as a break between corn crops. There is little nutritional difference between spring and winter beans, spring beans being just slightly higher in protein content and about 1 per cent lower in fibre. They contain in the region of 1.3 per cent oil.

Fig. 20 Field beans

The calcium:phosphorus ratio is 1:4.6, which represents a somewhat higher phosphorus content than in the oilseeds.

The protein content of the field bean is of a relatively good quality, having a higher lysine content than linseed but a lower level of methionine. It does not, however, compare for quality with soya bean meal.

Beans are a good source of energy, hence the saying 'full of beans'. They have a digestible energy value of 15.3 MJ/kg D.M., as compared with oats which have a value of 13.0.

Beans are very hard and therefore need cracking or grinding coarsely before feeding to horses; traditionally they should be stored for twelve months before feeding as, like linseed, immature samples can contain isothiocyanates. Whole beans can be used in mashes if they are boiled until soft, in which case they should be fed at the rate of a single handful per horse per day. Boiling also kills the mould spores which frequently affect field beans and which in turn can cause respiratory troubles.

Beans are very prone to attack by weevils, so samples should be examined carefully before purchase, to make sure that they are clean, shiny, and free from dust and holes.

Dried skim milk powder

Whole milk is too valuable a food for use other than human consumption and also generally too expensive to include in horse rations, therefore skim milk powder is most commonly used.

Milk powder supplements the protein level of rations where only poor-quality proteins such as those found in oats and hay are present in the diet. For this purpose it is second only to a high-grade white fish meal. It is very digestible and generally more palatable than other high-quality proteins. It contains lactose (milk sugar) which is the best source of carbohydrate for the young foal, but is deficient in iron.

Skim milk is what remains after the cream has been removed by centrifugal force, the remaining fat content being only in the region of 1 per cent, so most of the fat-soluble vitamins have also been removed with the cream. However, the other milk solids remain intact. The milk is usually dried either by a technique known as spray drying or by roller drying, the former method giving a product with a slightly higher nutritive value than the latter.

Milk powder is primarily used for orphan foals (see Chapter 12), foals at weaning time, and in the preparation of yearlings for the show-ring or sales. When milk powder is to be added to the diet, it is better to feed a product which has already been balanced for foals; or, failing this, a calf milk powder is better than the raw material, as it contains the required extra vitamins and minerals.

Raw eggs

Eggs are considered to have an ideal amino-acid composition, and this is taken as a standard by some authorities against which other proteins are compared.

However, egg white is known to contain a protein, avidin, which combines with the B vitamin biotin, preventing its absorption from the intestine. It is unlikely to have any effect on adult horses as biotin is produced in sufficiently large quanitities by the microbes in the large intestine, and in any case people do not usually feed eggs in quantity to horses. As young foals do not have any microbes in their intestines, it is recommended that not more than two eggs per day are given to these animals.

Blood eggs and cracked eggs can sometimes be bought from producers or packing stations at reduced rates and mixed in with the liquid portion of a mash. They form a valuable supplement to the grain ration for young horses and breeding stock.

Dried grass meal

The drying process does not alter the original composition of fresh grass except for a favourable change in the rate of solubility of the protein, therefore young leafy grass or lucerne, when dried, forms a very valuable protein supplement to the diet of stabled horses, but the quality of the sample does depend on the quality of the original grass. The carotene content, although initially high, tends to be destroyed gradually during storage; it may be as much as halved over a period of seven months if exposed to light and air. The vitamin D content is low as, unlike hay, the grass is not exposed to sunlight during drying.

Groundnut (peanut) meal could be fed in a normal ration, but as soya bean meal is a very much better source of protein the latter is to be recommended in preference. Also some samples of groundnut meal have been known to contain poisonous moulds.

Cottonseed meal tends to be dry and dusty; it also has a costive action and is therefore less suitable for inclusion in a straight ration. Some horses tend to develop colic on a costive diet, and dust can produce coughing and broken wind. The calcium:phosphorus ratio is nearly as high as that of bran, being 1:6, therefore supplementation with calcium would be very necessary. Some samples have been known to contain gossypol (a toxic substance).

Palm kernel meal tends to be rather dry and gritty and is therefore not palatable and so can only be included in cubes (nuts). It has a calcium:phosphorus ratio of 1:2.4, which is an improvement on cottonseed meal, but as it is high in fibre it is probably a more suitable feed for ruminants than for horses.

Coconut meal is often included in nuts as it will absorb up to 50 per cent of its own weight of molasses and so forms a useful binding medium. It does tend to be high in fibre and the protein is of relatively low quality, being deficient in both lysine and histidine.

Sunflower meal must be decorticated, but in spite of this treatment it has a high fibre content and is relatively indigestible.

Sesame meal is about 46 per cent crude protein and may be used as a direct replacement for groundnut meal.

Locust beans are the pods of the carob tree, *Ceratonia siliqua.* They are dark purple and glossy on the outside, contain a number of very hard indigestible seeds, and a sweet vein which runs along the top of the pod. The seeds, unless they are ground first, can collect in the stomach and cause colic.

Fish meal — there are two statutory definitions of fish meal in the British Isles; both state that it is '. . . a product obtained by drying and grinding or otherwise treating fish or waste fish, to which no other matter has been added'.

In addition, white fish meal must not contain more than 6 per cent oil and not more than 4 per cent salt. Only high-grade white fish meal should be used for horses.

Fish meal tends to be unpalatable and should be included in the ration only in small quantities. Due to its very satisfactory protein composition it is often included in horse nuts.

Fish meal is produced either by steam drying – in a steam-jacketed vessel – or by flame drying, in which case the meal is placed in a revolving drum and dried by hot air from a furnace.

The meal contains about 70 per cent crude protein, which is high in lysine, methionine, and tryptophan (see page 152). It is therefore a valuable supplement for oat and other cereal rations. It also contains growth factors known as Animal Protein Factors (APF), and is therefore a valuable addition to the diet of young horses and ponies. It is rich in minerals.

Dried brewer's yeast. This is a highly digestble protein feed (digestible crude protein 45 per cent), rich in most of the vitamins of the B complex, particularly B_6, but does not contain vitamin B_{12}. It helps utilisation and is therefore an ideal feed for horses with a high energy requirement, e.g. racehorses and lactating mares. It may be fed at the rate of two tablespoonsful per day or 5 lb (2 kg) per ton (tonne) of mix.

The old idea that excess dietary protein was harmful and caused protein poisoning was shown to be incorrect when vitamin B_{12} was discovered. The harmful effects were due to B_{12} deficiency. This vitamin is needed for the proper utilisation of protein; increasing the levels of protein in rations automatically increases the demand for B_{12}. If B_{12} is adequate and a well balanced ration is being fed there will be no ill effects from additional protein. Any surplus protein is broken down by the body and used as a source of energy.

7: The Effect of Feeding Urea to Horses

Urea, which should not be confused with urine as such, is an amide — the end product of nitrogen metabolism in mammals. It is equivalent to 290 per cent crude protein (46.6% N × 6.25), so is dangerous to include in a straight ration.

As protein foods (see Chapter 6) are generally the most expensive part of the ration, urea is sometimes used as a cheaper source of nitrogen in ruminant diets. However, low levels of urea may be given to *adult* horses with no ill effects. By law, if urea is included in a ration, the percentage must be stated on each bag. All cattle nuts, therefore, must be very carefully checked for the percentage of urea content before being fed to horses. It should also be borne in mind that urea, unlike protein foods, provides neither energy, vitamins nor minerals to the ration and on its own is unpalatable.

Dietary urea is hydrolysed by bacterial enzymes in the large intestine to ammonia (which is composed of hydrogen and nitrogen atoms). The ammonia is then 'trapped' by the microbes and the nitrogen it contains is utilised to build up microbial protein, which is eventually made available to the horse — it is thought — through the self-digestion of the microbes and the breakdown of the microbial protein into its constituent amino acids.

Ammonia as such is very toxic to all mammals; excess ammonia in the large intestine is rapidly absorbed through the gut wall, and as a safety device small quantities are converted to glutamine but larger quantities are converted back to urea by the liver. If the concentration of ammonia in the large intestine rises to very high levels, there is a rapid absorption through the gut wall but as the liver is unable to convert it all back to urea, the ammonia content in the peripheral blood rises to toxic levels. This occurs when urea is fed in excess to adult horses and ponies; 'protein poisoning' then follows.

In the young horse which has not developed a full complement of gut microbes, or in the case of adult horses receiving a course of oral antibiotics, there will be little, if any, hydrolysis of urea in the large intestine. Urea is a highly soluble substance, so, in these cases, all the urea will be absorbed through the small and large intestine walls and pass into the liver, where it will add to the naturally occurring urea. Urea which has not been broken down cannot be used to form amino acids so it is excreted in the urine, thus overtaxing and possibly damaging both the liver and the kidneys, with no nutritional benefit to the horse.

It has been found that urea is utilised best by the adult horse when the percentage of protein in the diet is low (i.e. below 10 per cent) and the soluble carbohydrate is high; then the microbes have no alternative supply of nitrogen and a good source of energy, e.g. in cereal diets. Utilisation is less effective when a low protein/high roughage diet is fed. Frequent small feeds have been observed to give better results than occasional large feeds. Where urea forms a substantial part of the dietary nitrogen, deficiencies of the sulphur-containing amino acids, such as methionine, will occur.

Excess urea from the liver is excreted in the urine and a small quantity is present in the saliva – the salivary urea being re-cycled. Amino-acid molecules constantly travel round within the horse's body moving from one tissue to the next; however, sometimes a particular amino acid liberated by one tissue is not taken up by any of the other tissues. In this case it is converted to urea and finally excreted in the urine.

The horse is able to utilise some urea but the amount is small when compared to natural protein supplements, such as soya bean meal; mature horses utilise more than young horses.

No harm will come from allowing *adult* horses access to cattle feed blocks containing urea. However, urea should not be included in horse rations until more research has been carried out and should never be used in rations intended for foals or valuable horses.

8: The Practical Aspects of Making Up Feeds

To be at all satisfactory any ration must fulfil certain conditions which can be summed up as follows:

1. The ration must be palatable — however nutritious and well balanced it might be, a ration is absolutely valueless if the horses or ponies will not eat it.

Palatability is principally controlled by the texture and taste of the individual foodstuffs and the amounts of each used. As far as possible a ration must be light and open; powdery ingredients tend to form a paste-like mass in the horse's mouth and are therefore less acceptable even if otherwise palatable. Some of the more common foods fed to horses which help to keep a ration open include:

Crushed oats	Flaked maize
Broad bran	Chop

'Heavy' ingredients include:

Soya bean meal	Grass meal
Milk powder	Fine bran or Thirds
Vitamin/mineral sup-	Boiled oats, barley or
plements	linseed
Soaked sugar beet pulp	

A well-constructed ration may contain some 'heavy' ingredients but these are counter-balanced in such a way that the over-all texture is light and palatable.

Like children, most horses need to be introduced to a new taste very gradually. Therefore, when introduced, new foodstuffs, however palatable they are known to be, should be added to the ration in minute amounts, well mixed in and the quantity increased very gradually every day until the full amount is being fed.

Occasionally it may be necessary to include an unpalatable ingredient such as cod liver oil. If this is firmly rejected by the horse, the good feeder uses his ingenuity to devise some method of getting the horse to take the substance. In this case, it might even mean squirting the oil onto the back of the horse's tongue with a syringe. It should be mentioned here that cod liver oil in its natural form will go rancid if kept for any length of time, particularly in hot weather. If fed in this condition it can lead to a vitamin E deficiency. Powdered forms, however, are available and these have relatively good keeping qualities and may be easier to administer. There are usually ways and means round most problems, if one applies a little imagination to the subject.

Palatability is also affected by the method of presentation – straight rations (not cubes) are usually improved by being fed slightly dampened; oats and bran, however good the samples are, tend to be dusty and will cause horses to breathe in dust while eating. In cold weather a warm feed is generally considered more acceptable than a cold one. Boiled food which has been allowed to go cold before feeding tends to become a less palatable, heavy mass. Conversely, a mash which is given too hot, will burn the horse's mouth and also put him off his food. Too much water should not be added to a feed as a high water content tends to produce solutes which have a detrimental effect on the gut microbes – the consistency of a wet feed should be crumbly.

Last but not least, palatability is greatly affected by the cleanliness or otherwise of the feeding and mixing utensils – nothing will put a horse off his food quicker than a dirty manger.

2. All the foodstuffs put into the ration must be free from

mould spores and dust in general, the dangers of which are fully described in Chapter 11.

3. The individual constituents of the ration must also be in good condition: hay, oats, beans, linseed etc, must have been stored for periods of between six and twelve months before feeding.

Hay — should be stored up to Christmas

Oats — should be stored up to Christmas

Beans — should be stored for twelve months

Linseed — should be stored for twelve months

The moisture content of oats stored in bulk should not exceed 14 per cent, otherwise the grain will tend to go rancid and mouldy; the only exception to this rule is propionic acid-treated grain. Only whole grain should be stored for any length of time and if kept in sacks, only those made of hessian should be used to allow for free ventilation. The oil in oats is unsaturated and rapidly goes rancid after the grain is crushed and consequently exposed to atmospheric oxygen. Crushed grain also tends to become mite-infested.

Crushed oats should be used within:

4 weeks in winter

2 weeks in summer

4. All the constituents of a ration must be very well mixed together before feeding. This is particularly important when the food is mixed in bulk for a number of horses, usually in a feed barrow. A badly mixed ration would mean that some horses could receive too much of one ingredient, too little of another and in consequence a badly balanced feed. It would also make it extremely easy for a horse to sort out the most palatable parts of his ration and leave the rest. Ideally the food should be turned over with a shovel (kept solely for this purpose) in the feed barrow, until it is evenly mixed.

5. Finely ground or milled ingredients should never be

given in a dry feed; they create far too much dust. The easiest way to deal with substances such as milk powder, dried grass and supplements, is to mix them with water and then add the liquid to the dry ingredients. This method ensures that they are fully dissolved or re-constituted before being added and this in turn ensures even distribution and palatability.

6. Syrupy substances, such as malt, cod liver oil or honey, mix best when they are dissolved in warm water. Powdered cod liver oil supplements or any other dry vitamin supplements are better fed in cold mashes so as not to destroy the vitamins they contain.

7. Sudden changes should never be made in a horse's diet — see Chapter 3. To obtain the maximum benefit from his food the horse should be maintained on the same diet all the time and any variations made very gradually — allowing plenty of time for the gut microbes to adapt themselves. All animals do best if they are kept to a particular routine — it does not matter if you give your horse his first feed at 10 am and his last feed at midnight, so long as you stick to these times.

Basically horses do best on *ad lib* diets but they need to be introduced to this system very carefully, otherwise, to start with, they will 'eat their heads off'. Most people compromise by feeding their horses three, if not four, times a day.

8. When buying the ingredients to make up horse rations, one must buy the very best obtainable — the quality of the individual constituents and their degree of digestibility will determine the over-all value of the final ration, so this is a most important factor. These days, by law, merchants are bound to declare the analysis of many of the products they sell.

As horses' food is obtained from growing matter, i.e. plant material or animal by-products such as milk, the exact analysis for each product will tend to vary slightly within certain limits. The analyses given in the Appendix are a guide to the average analysis of each foodstuff but should not be regarded as an exact breakdown of every sample which can be bought: these are affected by factors such as the soil, time of harvesting, weather conditions during growth and harvesting.

9. The art of feeding horses lies in giving each horse exactly what he needs to keep him in optimum condition, no more and no less.

Horses are usually kept for their athletic ability, therefore they should not be treated as a herd but must be fed as individuals. To obtain the very best results, their individual idiosyncrasies must be considered, up to a point.

In view of this individuality, only a general guide can ever be given for their feeding; beyond this, the good feeder adapts the basic ration for his own animal's needs.

10. Very bulky, high fibre/low energy diets are unsuitable for horses, as they have a comparatively high energy requirement and low bulk-intake capacity, which means that horses fed on poor-quality hay or straw, alone, cannot get enough energy from it to maintain their condition without supplementary feeding. Conversely, horses eat less if fed a high energy/low fibre diet, i.e. they automatically try to adjust their daily calorie intake to meet their requirements. This is the reason why horses will hardly touch their hay if given high-calorie rations, a fact which is utilised to advantage when feeding horses in hard work, e.g. racehorses (which have a very high calorie/low bulk requirement).

11. Any uneaten food must be removed from the manger, preferably within two hours of the last feed. Wet mashes should not be kept from one feed to the next, especially in hot weather, as they tend to go rancid, but dry feeds can be saved. Some horses will not eat up

all their food first thing in the morning but will clean it up after they have been out. Under these circumstances corn should be covered over, e.g. with a sack, until the horse returns, otherwise the birds will leave nothing but the husks and make a nasty mess of the manger at the same time. Other horses will eat up only when every-thing is quiet at night.

Mangers must be kept clean all the time.

9: Balancing Rations

Hay is the key to feeding horses and ponies. Good hay alone, fed *ad lib*, will provide the maintenance requirement of all adult animals not in work, breeding or lactating.

Concentrates are used to make good deficiencies in the hay; therefore, the better quality hay you use the less concentrates you will need and this will reduce your food bills.

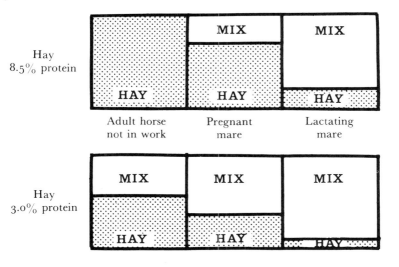

Fig. 21 Diagrams showing the difference good and poor hay make to the cost of keeping a horse. (A 15% C.P. mix was used in each case to balance the ration.)

As well as considering the nutritive value of foodstuffs one must also consider any other substances they could contain which may, during digestion and assimilation, affect the over-all value of the ration or actually be harmful to the horse.

Substances which fall into this category include cyanogenetic glycosides (found in samples of raw linseed), phytates (in bran), lignin (in straw and late cut hay), moulds (present in dusty hay and dangerous for both the feeder and the horse as they can cause 'Farmer's lung' in humans and broken wind, uterine infections or abortions in horses), toxins, hormones and nutrient inhibitors.

A nutrient is any feed constituent which aids in the support of animal life. The horse's nutrient requirements may be divided as follows:

protein requirement;
carbohydrate requirement;
fat requirement;
fibre requirement;
calcium:phosphorus ratio;
any other vitamin or mineral requirements.

Protein requirement

Protein requirements for the various classes of stock are given on page 26.

It is essential that the feeder knows the value of his hay before trying to formulate a balanced ration. Samples vary from as low as 2.5 per cent crude protein for poor field-cured hays to as high as 12 per cent crude protein for first quality barn-dried hays.

Barn-dried hay
1st quality	12% crude protein
2nd quality	10% crude protein
3rd quality	6–8% crude protein

Field-cured hay
   Italian ryegrass   2.5–6% crude protein
   Perennial ryegrass   5–8% crude protein
   Clover mix (leafy)   10–11% crude protein

Samples of hay may be sent to your local Ministry of Agriculture Nutritional Chemistry laboratory for analysis or some manufacturers of compound feeds will carry out the analysis for you free of charge if you use their product.

Look at your horse's protein requirement, then compare this with the analysis of your hay. If there is a protein deficiency in the hay it must be made good with nuts or concentrate mix.

When feeding *adult* horses it is only necessary to look at the *quantity* of protein required.

When feeding youngstock and broodmares in the last 90 days of gestation and during lactation it is also necessary to select foods which will provide a satisfactory level of amino acids. Those most commonly selected for this purpose are:

    Extracted or full fat soya bean meal
    Skimmed milk powder
    High-grade white fish meal

The percentage crude protein should, by law, be given on the bag of coarse mix, cubes, nuts or protein food when you buy it. An approximate analysis of most foodstuffs can be found in the Appendix (page 146).

According to the Fertilizers and Feeding Stuffs (Amendment) Regulations 1976, the following must be declared for these feeds:

    Lucerne or grass meal (artificially dried) – amount of protein
    Dried molassed beet pulp – amounts of sugar and fibre respectively

Flaked maize — amounts of oil and protein respectively

Soya meal — amounts of oil and protein respectively

Treacle or molasses — amount of sugar

Bran — amount of fibre

The law allows a certain latitude either side of the figures stated and this varies slightly with the different foodstuffs.

When you have more than one source of protein to choose from the value is found by taking the one with the best amino acid 'picture' and simply dividing the percentage protein into the price per ton. This gives the unit value of the crude protein, although the price becomes less important where high-value stock is concerned.

All grain is deficient in lysine, therefore, using the amino acid breakdown charts in the Appendix, a foodstuff which is particularly well endowed with this amino acid should be chosen from the list of proteins to balance a normal oat and bran ration for youngstock and broodmares. As a quick 'rule of thumb' guide, the value of any protein can be assessed by looking at the lysine figure. Only a little research has been done on the other amino acids, so it is widely assumed that if the lysine content is correct then the rest will also be balanced. If synthetic lysine is added to correct the diet, a lower protein ration can be fed in most cases.

Diets deficient in protein can lead to a generally lowered wellbeing and antibody response to disease (Miller, 1976). If, for instance, your hay is a very good sample and has an analysis of 8.5 per cent crude protein or over, it can safely be fed to all adult horses and ponies which are not in work, without additional concentrates. If, on the other hand, it has an analysis less than 8.5 per cent crude protein, a concentrate mix must be fed

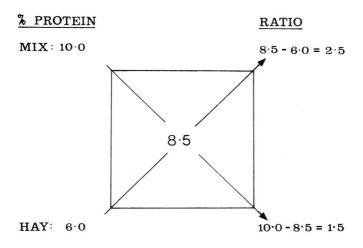

% PROTEIN

MIX: 10·0

HAY: 6·0

RATIO

8·5 - 6·0 = 2·5

10·0 - 8·5 = 1·5

TOTAL 2·5 + 1·5 = 4·0

FOOD REQUIREMENT = 2·5 % OF LIVEWEIGHT = "X"

AMOUNT OF MIX = "X" x $\frac{2·5}{4}$

to balance the ration. The amount needed of each can be worked out as follows:

> Hay = 6 per cent crude protein (for example)
> Nuts mix = 10 per cent crude protein (for example)
> Horse requires 8.5 per cent crude protein

You therefore need to feed 2.5 parts of nuts to 1.5 parts hay. The weight of food is related to the body weight of the horse. Adult horses eat on average 2.5 per cent of their body weight in food per day. Youngstock, broodmares in the last ninety days of gestation and during lactation eat 3.0 per cent of their body weight in food per day. The following figures are given as an approximate guide:

Up to 12.2 h.h.	approx 16 lb (7.2 kg) per day
12.2 to 14.2 h.h.	approx 21 lb (9.4 kg) per day
14.2 to 16.0 h.h.	approx 28 lb (12.6 kg) per day
over 16.0 h.h.	approx 32 lb (14.4 kg) per day

Assuming our horse's food requirement is 12.6 kg, then the weight of nuts he should be given each day is:

$$\frac{12.6 \times 2.5}{(2.5 + 1.5)} = 7.9 \text{ nuts per day}$$

Given the choice most horses will eat corn or nuts in preference to hay, so although the calculated hay requirement is 12.6 – 7.9 = 4.7 kg per day, in practice it is better to offer the hay *ad lib*.

Obviously not everyone likes to use nuts, cubes or ready mixed coarse feeds. Those who like to construct their own rations also need to know the crude protein value of their mix in order to feed a balanced diet.

The following list is given as a guide to the percentage of each ingredient which can be included in a ration for horses.

	% air dry feed	
Oats	90	
Barley	15	(fed cooked)
Wheat	0	
Rye	0	
Maize	30	(flaked or cracked)
Field beans	10	(boiled or cracked)
Linseed	10	(fed cooked)
Wheat bran	10	
Dried molassed sugar beet pulp	15	(fed soaked)
Molasses	10	
Soya bean meal	15	
Carrots	75	
Fish meal	10	

Dried skimmed milk	15
Dried yeast	0.2
Grass meal	50 (fed damp)

With reference to the above list and to the protein tables in the appendix, the following ration might be constructed for a horse in work:

% fed	food	% crude protein	
85	oats	11 (85×11) =	935
5	bran	17 (5×17) =	85
10	grass meal	16 (10×16) =	160
100			1180

Therefore % crude protein for the mix is:

$$\frac{1180}{100} = 11.8\% \text{ crude protein}$$

The same ration can be adapted to meet the needs of a lactating mare, foal or yearling by substituting soya bean meal for grass meal to raise both the quantity and quality of the protein:

% fed	food	% crude protein	
85	oats	11 (85×11) =	935
5	bran	17 (5×17) =	85
10	extracted soya bean meal	50 (10×50) =	500
100			1520

Therefore % crude protein of the mix is:

$$\frac{1520}{100} = 15.2\,\% \text{ crude protein}$$

When working out your own ration weigh each ingredient separately, add up the total weight of the mix fed each day, then the percentage of each foodstuff can be calculated by dividing the weight of the mix into the weight of each food and multiplying the results by 100.

The crude protein figures can be found on pages 149-52.

Energy requirement

The horse's energy requirement is related to its condition. Some people are good feeders but most tend to over-feed their horses which is both costly and detrimental to the horse's health, performance and lifespan. A few people over-horse themselves and are then frightened to feed their animals well; some may be just too mean to spend money on food.

The horse gets energy from his food in the following ways:

1. The breakdown of starch and simple sugars in the small intestine
2. The microbial breakdown of fibre in the hind gut
3. Any excess protein in the diet
4. Any fat or oil in the diet.

One cannot lay down hard and fast rules for energy as a number of factors can alter the requirement. These include environment, the individual horse (his genetic makeup and temperament), presence of subclinical disease, such as worm parasites, and work.

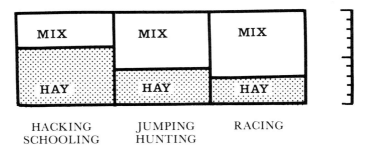

Fig. 22 Increase the concentration of energy in the diet as the horse's work becomes more intense.

Work increases the horse's energy requirement. This, as with the other factors, is met by altering the ration of grain (or concentrate mix) to hay, as shown in Fig. 22, or by increasing the energy concentration of the mix.

Common foodstuffs high in starch energy are oats, barley and maize.

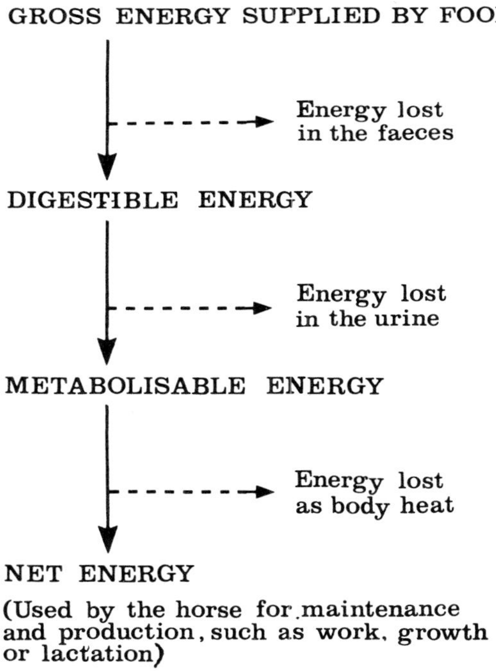

GROSS ENERGY SUPPLIED BY FOOD

- - - - - - → **Energy lost in the faeces**

DIGESTIBLE ENERGY

- - - - - - → **Energy lost in the urine**

METABOLISABLE ENERGY

- - - - - - → **Energy lost as body heat**

NET ENERGY
(Used by the horse for maintenance and production, such as work, growth or lactation)

Fig. 23 How energy is utilised by the horse

Common foodstuffs high in fibre energy include hay, dried grass or lucerne, bran, dried sugar beet pulp.

Cooking is thought to increase the digestible energy of grain by 3 per cent, since it makes more available to enzyme action in the small intestine. Some foods contain a more highly digestible fibre than others, for example sugar beet pulp. Chopping and milling increase digestibility slightly and intake of hay by 14 per cent.

Rations designed to increase a horse's body weight should contain a high proportion of starch foods. For horses in light work foods with a highly digestible fibre content should be selected, such as molassed sugar beet pulp. Horses in very poor condition should be offered cooked grain.

The amount fed will depend on the size of the horse and the value of the hay. Even if a high-quality hay is used some of this, plus a grain ration, should be included to increase the starch energy level of the diet of thin horses.

The following is an example of a fattening ration:

% fed	food	% crude protein	
20	boiled oats	11 (20 × 11) =	220
10	bran	17 (10 × 17) =	170
15	molassed sugar beet pulp (before soaking)	10 (15 × 10) =	150
15	rolled cooked barley	11 (15 × 11) =	165
10	flaked maize	11 (10 × 11) =	110
30	grass meal	16 (30 × 16) =	480
100			1295

Therefore % crude protein of the mix $= \dfrac{1295}{100} = 12.95\%$

When root crops or silage form part of the ration calculate the percentage fed on their dry matter content. If they form a large part of the diet, their water content may restrict intake and lead to weight loss.

Fibre requirement

This is also part of the horse's energy requirement as the breakdown of fibre by the gut microbes releases energy for the horse's metabolism.

Foals up to the age of seven months should be given a

Probably the most common fault of all: many people really enjoy feeding horses and get a thrill out of seeing them become fat, but over-fatness does not constitute good feeding and is very bad for the horse's health

relatively low-fibre diet, as until they are at least seven months old they have not developed a full complement of gut microbes and are therefore incapable of dealing with quantities of fibrous food.

Since fibre passes undigested into the large intestine, high-fibre diets cause pot-bellies, which are undesirable in horses doing fast work. Also, the energy derived from the breakdown of starch is more efficiently utilised by the body than the energy derived from the break-down of fibre.

However, some fibre is required in the diet, otherwise the natural balance of the gut microbes will be upset and digestive troubles may occur. It can form up to 1.5 per cent of the horse's body weight in a diet or 1 per cent for young horses and those in hard work. Lack of fibre in the diet can be a cause of wood chewing.

People imagine they will never be able to control their horses if they feed them well. This too is not good for the horse

Calcium:phosphorus ratio

As most of the foods we give our horses are too high in phosphates a daily calcium supplement is necessary to correct the diet if conditions such as rickets, osteomalacia, osteoporosis, epiphysitis, splints, curbs etc. are to be avoided.

The calcium and phosphorus levels of a mix can be calculated as follows:

% fed	foodstuff	% calcium	% phosphorus
70	oats	0.1 (70 × 0.1) = 7.0	0.35 (70 × 0.35) = 24.5
10	bran	0.14 (10 × 0.14) = 1.4	0.84 (10 × 0.84) = 8.4
5	soya	0.20 (5 × 0.20) = 1.0	0.60 (5 × 0.60) = 3.0
15	grass meal	0.95 (15 × 0.95) = 14.3	0.35 (15 × 0.35) = 5.2
100		23.7	41.1

Which means there is 23.7/100 = 0.24% calcium in the mix and 41.1/100 = 0.41% phosphorus in the mix.

Calcium:phosphorus ratio = 0.24:0.41

= 1:1.7

Desired minimum calcium:phosphorus ratio = 1:1

More food energy is needed in cold weather — good quality hay should be fed *ad lib* together with concentrates

As the phosphorus content is 0.41 per cent, the minimum acceptable calcium figure is 0.41 per cent (i.e. to give a 1 : 1 ratio). Because a wider ratio is desired, and to allow for variations in quality of feed, a higher value for calcium — say 0.50 per cent in this case — can be taken and also provides a safety margin.

Therefore target calcium content of mix = $\underline{0.50\%}$
actual calcium content of mix = $\underline{0.24\%}$
difference = $\underline{0.26\%}$

therefore 100 lb (kg) mix requires the addition of 0.26 lb (kg) calcium.

Assuming feeding-grade ground limestone can be purchased containing 36 per cent calcium, then 36 lb (kg) calcium are contained in 100 lb (kg) limestone flour. Thus 0.26 lb (kg) calcium is contained in:

$$\frac{100 \times 0.26}{36} \text{ lb (kg) limestone flour}$$

= 0.722 lb (kg) limestone flour

Therefore, each 100 lb (kg) mix should be supplemented with 0.722 lb (kg) limestone flour.

If the daily ration for a horse is 16 lb (7.25 kg) mix, then this should be supplemented with limestone flour, calculating the amount as follows:

$$\frac{16 \times 0.722}{100} \text{ lb limestone flour}$$

= 0.1155 lb
= (16 × 0.1155 oz)
= 1.85 oz (i.e. approx. 2 oz per day)

In metric terms 7.25 kg mix should be supplemented with

$$\frac{7.25 \times 0.722}{100} \text{ kg limestone flour}$$

= 0.0523 kg limestone flour
= 52 g limestone flour

Horses and ponies require a calcium:phosphorus ratio of not less than 1:1 and young horses can be allowed a 1.7:1.0 ratio. It is better to err on the side of giving too much calcium rather than too little — any excess will be passed out in the faeces or urine.

The most common calcium supplements used are:

- (i)   Ground limestone, containing 38 per cent calcium
- (ii) Calcium lactate, containing 13 per cent calcium
- (iii) Calcium gluconate, containing 9 per cent calcium
- (iv) Dicalcium phosphate, 23.6 per cent calcium and 17.9 per cent phosphorus
- (v)   Steamed bone flour, 38.5 per cent calcium, 13.5 per cent phosphorus, 0.35 per cent magnesium and 0.47 per cent sodium.

Calcium lactate and calcium gluconate are highly soluble:

Calcium lactate has 20:1 solubility in water

Calcium gluconate has 30:1 solubility in water.

All horses and ponies during the winter months and others stabled all the time, should be given a vitamin A and D supplement in their diet such as:

- (i)   Cod liver oil
- (ii) Cod liver oil and malt
- (iii) Halibut liver oil and malt
- (iv) Powdered or liquid vitamin supplement

Essential fatty acid requirement

Essential fatty acids are those the body is not able to synthesise or cannot synthesise adequately to meet its needs. Linoleic and arachidonic acid are the most important; arachidonic acid can be synthesised in the body from linoleic acid.

Polyunsaturated fatty acids are considered to be important for the maintenance of a healthy skin and hair coat. With other species a lack of fat or essential fatty acids causes a slower growth rate, an enlarged fatty liver, hair loss, dandruff-like conditions, lowered reproduction and lactation and eventual death.

It is unlikely that a deficiency will occur with practical, well-balanced horse rations. In the pig, the requirement for linoleic acid is 0.22 per cent of the ration. Extracted protein supplements contain low levels of linoleic acid, for instance solvent extracted soya bean meal contains only 0.4 per cent whereas full fat soya bean meal contains 10 per cent. Oats contain 1.5 per cent.

The interesting document below is reproduced by kind

Daily allowance of Provender for Horses. November 1904 —

	I Corn	Oats	Bran	Hay	Total
Cart Horses "	13	1	1	14	29
Float "	12	1	1	12	26
Black "	8	1	1	12	22
Cab "	10	1	1	12	24

Average per horse. per day. 25·1 lbs —

	1904. lbs	1905 lbs	1906. lbs.
I Corn .	11·20	8·32	9·38
Oats .	1·33	2·89	3·22
Bran .	·70	1·22	·88
Hay .	11·04	12·66	15·51
	24·24 lb	25·10 lb	28·99 lb

permission of the late G. Allup Esq. of Whittingham Hall, Preston, Lancashire. It is interesting to see that these horsemen recognised the high energy value of Indian corn (flaked maize) which was relatively cheap at the time. This is reflected in the quantities they gave the various classes of horse, with the black (funeral) horses receiving the least. The horses must have looked fat and well on this diet but the feeders could not have realised the significance and possible dangers of the low calcium, high phosphorus ratio (approximately 1:8) of the diet they were giving and the possible reduction in length of sound working life of the horses.

10: Conditions Associated with Errors in Diet

Bran Disease

Otherwise known as 'Big Head' or Osteofibrosis. This condition is seen in horses and ponies fed on diets which are very high in bran. The high level of phosphate in the diet causes the horse to draw on the calcium reserves in its bones, which in turn tend to become brittle. The disease is characterised by a swelling of the bones of the lower jaw, hence the name 'Big Head'.

Treatment consists of balancing the diet by eliminating the bran, replacing it with, say, grass meal and feeding a calcium supplement.

Choking

A horse's gullet (oesophagus) is only about 2 in. in diameter, therefore great care must be taken in the preparation of food, to ensure that none will get stuck after being swallowed.

Carrots must always be cut lengthways.

Any food which is inclined to swell in the presence of moisture must be well soaked in water overnight before feeding. Sugar beet nuts are particularly dangerous, as they can swell and block the gullet completely. Unsoaked dried sugar beet pulp will also cause colic.

Signs of choking include arching of the neck and trying to be sick. Food particles, froth and saliva return down the nostrils. The horse appears distressed and usually refuses to eat or drink.

This condition should not be confused with grass

96

sickness which can also produce symptoms of food particles returning down the nostrils.

Colic

Colic is just a word meaning pain in the abdomen. It can, therefore, be a symptom of a number of different conditions, some of which are:
1. Impaction of food in the large colon, which may be due to errors in diet — low water/high fibre diets; sudden changes in diet; imbalanced or poor-quality rations; errors in management, regarding the relationship of work, rest, watering and feeding; poorly chewed food, due to sharp teeth or mouth injuries;
2. Diarrhoea — due to alimentary tract infections, see also page 98;
3. Gas in the intestines — due to ingested food fermenting or bacterial toxins;
4. Intestinal worms and their effects;
5. Abscesses or tumours in the gut wall;
6. Twisted gut;
7. Tears in the gut wall.

Pain is the main feature of colic and the symptoms are just the individual horse's reactions to this pain.

An affected horse becomes restless, stops feeding, walks round in circles, paws the ground and kicks up at its stomach. It usually turns its head to look at its flanks with a worried expression on its face and breaks out in a sweat.

In order to try to find a comfortable position in which to stand or lie, the horse will sometimes stretch himself out, sit up like a dog, roll or lie on his back. In severe cases the horse may throw himself about violently and be in great danger of injuring both himself and his attendants.

Most commonly the pain is caused by stretching of the gut wall, due either to the formation of gases or to the impaction of food in one particular area of the bowel. Normally the food is propelled along the gut by means of muscular contractions, known as peristalsis; but sometimes these contractions cease or become over-active, then colic results.

As colic is only a symptom of several conditions, the veterinary surgeon has the problem of establishing the exact cause. He will usually attempt to find the cause, then control the pain and prescribe treatment.

Simple blockages may be treated with purgatives, such as medicinal paraffin. Flatulent or gassy colics may respond to suitable anti-spasmodic drugs and antibiotics. Surgery is sometimes essential in cases of twisted gut. Contrary to popular belief, twisting is not usually the result of allowing the horse to roll, but is caused by part of the gut ceasing to function and so becoming twisted round by the rest of the gut which is still active. The pain caused by this twist makes the horse roll – not vice versa.

In all cases of colic it is better to call in your veterinary surgeon rather than try to treat the horse yourself, as the wrong treatment will only tend to aggravate the condition.

The following symptoms are usually regarded as serious:
1. Continuous pain for periods in excess of six hours;
2. Patchy sweating but the ears feel cold;
3. Rapid pulse rate – this can best be felt just under the left jaw bone where a large artery runs over the edge of the bone (a normal pulse rate is about forty to the minute);
4. Straining;
5. Drum-like distension of the flanks;
6. Brick red mucous membranes.

Diarrhoea

This can be a symptom of several different diseases, errors in feeding or worm infestations.

A nutritional diarrhoea can best be differentiated from a diarrhoea caused by an infectious condition by checking the horse's temperature. This should fall somewhere within the range of $100°F-101.5°F$.

Most foals will suffer from diarrhoea at some period before weaning, often when the mare first comes in-season after foaling. This is thought to be due to changes in the composition of the mare's milk at this time, but the ingestion of poor-quality high-bulk feed, such as inferior hay, before the foal's digestive tract is capable of dealing with these fibrous substances, may play a part. The foaling heat scour usually stops quite naturally soon after the mare stops being in-season. The foal does not normally go 'off suck' or show any other symptoms of illness but this 'natural' scour can weaken the foal and make it more susceptible to infectious scours at this time, which can be much more serious.

Nutritional scours in older horses can be due to such factors as:

1. Feeding immature samples of hay or oats;
2. Giving rations which are too high in protein for the particular horse's needs so producing an excess of undigested protein in the hind gut, or suddenly increasing the level of protein in the diet;
3. Feeding mashes which are too wet or over-dampening feeds, particularly bran;
4. Giving sulphonamide drugs or antibiotics by mouth;
5. Making very sudden changes in a horse's diet. This can also be one of the predisposing causes of the usually fatal condition known as Colitis X.

Nutritional scours, as well as weakening the horse, represent a waste of food, as only partial digestion takes place.

Laminitis

This is the term used to describe inflammation of the sensitive laminae inside the horse's foot. All inflammation produces swelling but due to the rigid structure of the hoof wall, very little swelling can take place, therefore the horse is in great pain. The laminae tend to separate from the wall of the hoof, the pedal bone tilts downwards and in chronic cases may even penetrate the sole. The hoof develops a concaved, ridged appearance (see Fig. 24).

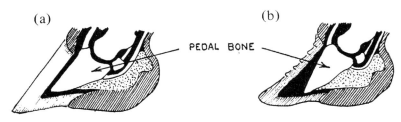

(a)   (b)

PEDAL BONE

Fig. 24 (a) Normal foot; (b) foot affected by laminitis

Laminitis has long been thought to be due to over-feeding and under-work; it is particularly common in small ponies. Recent research has tended to confirm that high protein diets and diets which produce high levels of lactic acid as the end product of microbial fermentation in the large intestine are mainly to blame. Other factors include letting a horse's toes grow too long, stress factors, e.g. after foaling, and access to an *ad lib* supply of food, say, after a horse has strayed into the feed house.

The fore feet are more commonly affected by inflammation than the hind feet. Characteristically the horse stands with as much weight as possible on his heels, in an effort to relieve the pain. If he is lying down, he may be very reluctant to rise and will show signs of pain in the expression on his face and the fact that he may sweat profusely. The affected feet will feel hot. The condition may be acute or chronic.

Treatment begins by correcting the diet, initially to hay and water alone, calling in your veterinary surgeon and being guided by his advice and treatment for the individual case.

Lymphangitis

This is typically a hot painful swelling which occurs most often in the hind legs, but can equally well occur in the front legs, or under the abdomen. In the legs the swelling can extend right up as far as the stifle or the forearm, ending in a distinct ridge. After twenty-four to seventy-two hours, serum escapes through the skin in bad cases and runs down the leg. At this stage the swelling usually starts to go down.

At the first possible opportunity the horse should receive gentle exercise. The diet must be reduced to hay and water only, from the first moment the symptoms appear. Susceptible horses should not be given very high starch or protein diets, and the relationship of work to food must be very carefully regulated.

As with Laminitis, a badly balanced diet can be a predisposing factor in producing this condition.

Lymphangitis can be primarily an infectious condition involving the fluid drainage (lymphatic) system of the leg and needs urgent treatment by a veterinary surgeon.

Nettle Rash

Otherwise known as Urticaria, this is a condition characterised by flat raised areas almost anywhere on the horse's skin. It is the result of an allergic reaction to some protein, which can be anything from an insect bite to a dietary protein.

Treatment consists of calling your veterinary surgeon who may wish to prescribe antihistamines, and trying to find the cause of the allergy.

Round joints

These are the result of inflammation affecting the growth plates (epiphyses) at the ends of the limb bones in young horses and foals. They are usually caused by trauma or errors in diet such as an imbalance in the calcium:phosphorus ratio, or lack of vitamin D. They occur when the energy level of the diet is too high, producing heavy-topped animals, thus exerting unnatural pressure on the epiphyses, especially when the ground is hard.

The swellings can be hot and tender and the affected animal will sometimes go lame. In other cases they will appear firm and cold. 'Knobbly fetlocks' are quite commonly seen in thoroughbred foals between three and six months of age, and these usually come right with time.

Swellings affecting the knee and hock joints are found in yearlings and two-year-olds, i.e. up to 2½ years old when the epiphyses are usually closed.

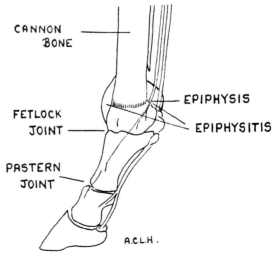

CANNON BONE

EPIPHYSIS

FETLOCK JOINT

EPIPHYSITIS

PASTERN JOINT

A.C.L.H.

Fig. 25 (a) Round joints (fetlock)

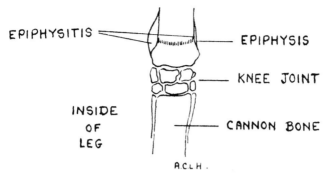

Fig. 25 (b) Round joints (knee)

Treatment usually consists of correcting the diet. Your veterinary surgeon may wish to take blood samples to determine if any gross calcium:phosphorus imbalance is present. Exercise must be restricted and affected animals must be put on soft going.

Bran should not be given to affected horses as this is very high in phosphates. Calcium lactate, carbonate or steamed bone flour should be added to the diet and the protein level of the ration reduced.

Horses which are in show condition or being prepared for sale and those which are conformationally heavy-topped are most prone to this condition. Their leg joints must be watched very carefully and their diet and management adjusted accordingly if round joints are to be avoided.

A horse's or pony's appetite is usually taken as a 'barometer' of his health. The degree to which an animal loses his appetite can be taken as a 'rule of thumb' guide to the severity of his illness, likewise an increase in appetite after an illness is usually taken as an indication that the horse is recovering.

During illness most animals receive little, if any,

exercise, therefore their diets should be reduced accordingly. A slightly higher level of protein may however be given after accidents and operations to help restore the damaged muscle tissue.

Horses or ponies which are off their feed should be tempted with anything they are known to enjoy normally, such as pieces of carrot or apple. Very small appetising feeds should be made up and any uneaten food *must* be removed from the manger at least one hour before the next feed is given, otherwise the horse will tend not to feel hungry.

Sick horses must never be allowed to drink from buckets or troughs used by other horses, nor should food rejected by a sick horse ever be offered to any other horse.

11: Feeding Broken-winded Horses

Broken wind or chronic emphysema is the result of a horse becoming allergic to its surroundings. Usually this takes the form of a chronic bronchitic asthma and is induced by dust containing mould spores from hay, straw and food. This causes a breakdown of the air-cells in the lungs, reducing the area through which the normal exchange of gases takes place. The affected horse then has great difficulty when expelling air from its lungs, hence the characteristic double expiratory lift of the broken-winded horse.

Once established, this condition is incurable but a lot can be done to prolong the horse's useful working life by careful management and feeding.

The first and most important thing is to eliminate all dust and so also mould spores from the atmosphere of the stable or loose-box. Brush down any cobwebs. Remove all traces of straw from the floor and change over to some other form of bedding material such as peat-moss litter, shavings or shredded paper.

If the horse is normally housed in a cage loose-box, it is necessary to move him into a conventional loose-box away from other horses. Alternatively, it means changing the bedding of all horses in the building, otherwise mould spores will remain in the atmosphere.

As far as feeding goes, the horse can usefully be given complete horse cubes which are obtainable from most horse-feed manufacturers together with exact feeding instructions. These eliminate the necessity for feeding hay and are probably the easiest answer to the problem, especially in a busy yard.

For the owner who prefers to maintain the traditional method of feeding, it means dampening every feed no matter what it is, to eliminate all dust particles.

Any hay must be very well soaked before feeding; it is not sufficient merely to sprinkle water over the top as the moisture must *really* penetrate to the centre of the pile. The easiest way to do this is to use a well-tarred hay net (the tar will prevent the net from rotting too quickly) and a water trough or household dustbin. You will also need to drive a stout nail or hook into the wall near the trough about five feet from the ground.

Fill the hay net as usual, but about four hours before you need to use it place it in the water trough and making quite certain that it is completely immersed, leave it to soak. About half an hour before feeding, lift the net out of the water and hang it from the nail to drain; leave it there until it has stopped dripping before tying it up in the loose-box or stable. The water in the trough should be changed regularly as it soon becomes brown and ferments, particularly in hot weather. When re-filling the net discard any uneaten hay. Haylage is recommended for broken-winded horses.

Mashes (see Chapter 13) are the ideal way of feeding broken-winded horses, otherwise (as already stated) all dry feeds apart from horse cubes must be dampened before feeding — only enough water should be added to kill the dust not make the ration sloppy. The final consistency should be crumbly.

Plenty of ventilation must be allowed at all times, otherwise broken-winded horses can become very distressed. This is of particular importance in hot weather, when affected horses are probably better left out both day and night, as problems can arise if they are brought into a stuffy loose-box on a hot summer evening.

12: Feeding Orphan Foals

For the purposes of this chapter we will define an orphan foal as one which for any reason has been deprived of its mother's milk and for which no foster mother can be found. In other words, any foal which will have to be reared by hand if it is to survive.

Initially the foal must receive some colostrum (first milk). Unlike the human baby, when it is born the foal has no resistance to disease; it obtains this resistance only through drinking the colostrum and absorbing the antibodies it contains. As this ability to absorb antibodies ceases soon after birth, it is essential that the foal receives colostrum within the first twenty-four hours of life, so that it can develop resistance to most of the diseases with which it is likely to come in contact.

In areas where there are several owners of single brood-mares, it is a very good idea if an arrangement can be made between them to collect a little colostrum from each mare as she foals (providing the mare has not produced an haemolytic foal), date it and store in a sterilised polythene bottle in a deep-freeze. Deep-frozen colostrum will keep from the end of one foaling season to the beginning of the next and only needs warming to blood heat before feeding. The colostrum is then immediately available for any orphan foal or for a foal from a mare which has run her milk before foaling.

To milk a mare, first wash your hands well and sponge the mare's udder with warm water. Smear a little Vaseline on her teats before you start and use your finger and thumb to draw the milk into a clean polythene jug. A second person should hold the mare unless she is very quiet. You will need to draw only about half a pint of colostrum from one teat while the foal is sucking the other teat.

Colostrum from donkeys can be given in the absence of mare's colostrum, but cow's colostrum is not recommended as, apart from the difference in composition between the two milks, it is unlikely, unless the cow has been living in close proximity to horses, that her coloostrum will contain any of the antibodies which will give the foal resistance to normal equine diseases.

If it is absolutely impossible to obtain any colostrum in time, your veterinary surgeon must be called so that he can give the foal some substitute colostrum and antibiotic or serum injections.

All foals must receive some form of milk for at least the first four months of their lives if they are going to survive. For the first six weeks the foal must be fed every two hours, both day and night. Then the length of time between feeds can be gradually increased: every three hours after six weeks, increasing to every four hours at twelve weeks. Foals cannot be treated like calves but must be fed little and often: overfeeding at any one time will make a foal ill.

At first the foal should be fed from a bottle fitted with a lamb's rubber teat, obtainable from most agricultural chemists and measuring about 4 in. × 1 in.

Milk is also an ideal food for bacteria (germs), so any bottles, teats and mixing utensils used for feeding must be kept absolutely clean and sterilised between each feed. Sterilisation can be carried out with boiling water or by using a dairy chemical or nursery sterilising agent, such as hypochlorite, in which case care should be taken to make sure that the surfaces to be sterilised are absolutely clean before treatment.

If the equipment is not sterilised after each feed, the

foal will probably start to scour and become quite ill. To avoid digestive upsets the milk should always be fed at the same temperature, preferably blood heat. To achieve this it is often better if the same person feeds the foal all the time wherever possible. Unused milk should be thrown away and never re-warmed. Milk should not be prepared and left exposed to the atmosphere for any length of time before feeding, as it easily becomes contaminated.

A satisfactory substitute for mare's milk can be made up easily in the following way:

> 2 tablespoonfuls of lime-water (*NOT* lime juice cordial), obtainable from most chemists
>
> 4 tablespoonfuls of glucose (powder)
>
> Make up to 1 pint with warm cow's milk

Goat's milk, when it is available, will give better results than cow's milk in the above recipe.

An alternative method of rearing foals by hand is to use Ostermilk No. 2 at the following rates:

> From birth to about 1 month, or according to size of foal (per feed):
>
> > 4 measures of Ostermilk
> >
> > 2 measures of glucose
> >
> > 8 fluid oz water
>
> From about 1 month to weaning (per feed):
>
> > 10 measures of Ostermilk
> >
> > 4 measures of glucose
> >
> > 1 pint of water

The Ostermilk should be mixed to a paste with a little cold water until there are no lumps left, then hot water added and the temperature adjusted to blood heat. Too much liquid will cause the foal to develop a pot-belly.

Should the foal start scouring due to a digestive upset, as with bucket-reared calves the milk substitute should be withdrawn and replaced by glucose and water only for a day or two.

Ostermilk is really designed for human babies and is a rather expensive method of rearing foals by hand through to weaning. There are two mare's milk replacers on the market formulated to the exact requirements of orphan foals, and these should be used in preference to others.

The original product, named Equilac, is available from Horse Requisites, Newmarket, Suffolk who have a twenty-four-hour answering service on (0638) 664619. Volac also introduced a specialist product in 1980 called Horse Power mare's milk replacer — details of your nearest stockist can be obtained by telephoning Arrington (Herts.) 363 or Limerick 40374.

Feeding instructions are included on all bags of milk replacer but it is wise to consult your veterinary surgeon in the case of premature or very weak foals.

Most foals are born with a well-developed suck reflex and those which are slow in this respect will usually develop the desire to suck soon after getting to their feet. Ideally the foal should have its first feed within two hours of birth and certainly not later than four hours. Warm up 6 fl. oz. colostrum or if none is available call your veterinary surgeon. Colostrum must be given once every three hours for the first twelve hours. In cases where the mare dies foaling, some colostrum can usually be drawn from her udder before she dies, and this can be given to the foal. If you have no milk or equipment, it is better to wait until the shops open in the morning than risk upsetting the foal with a home-made substitute.

To get a foal to drink from the bottle, first make sure that the hole in the rubber teat is large enough to allow a good flow of milk to escape. Give the foal a taste of the milk by squirting a little into its mouth — the teat can be smeared with honey. This should awaken its suck reflex. If this fails, make sure your hands are clean, run a little milk on to your fingers and get the foal to suck them, then gradually substitute the teat for your fingers. Unless he is lying down, it is better to get the foal's hindquarters into a corner; this will give you the maximum control. If the foal does not start to suck soon, squeeze some milk out of the end of the teat into his mouth, until he finally gets the idea. When he gets hungry he will soon start to suck without much trouble.

It is best if the orphan foal can be encouraged to eat some form of solid food as soon as possible. Most foals will nibble a little warm bran mash from your fingers the day after they are born; something warm and wet will encourage them more than a dry feed. Therefore a mixture of a little bran, boiled linseed, rolled oats and flaked maize is highly suitable. Once the foal is beginning to eat, he should be introduced to nuts.

Ad lib feeding of nuts is perhaps to be preferred, as the foal can then help itself whenever it wishes. This is a particularly useful method of rearing for all foals, especially where the owner goes out to work each day. A boiled barley and linseed mash containing crushed oats, extracted soya bean meal, calcium and vitamins A and D can be given every night, to add some variety to the diet. The foal must also receive *ad lib* good-quality hay and water.

A foal which is to be hand-reared must be put into a clean loose-box — one which has not had a sick (particularly a scouring) foal in it that season. If possible it should be given a companion, otherwise it will feel very lonely and may not thrive. A quiet sheep, goat or big dog is suitable. Make sure the foal is kept warm. In cold weather an infra-red lamp may be necessary, or a rug can be made out of a woollen jumper, putting the foal's front legs through the arms.

Foals develop social attachments during the first week or so of their lives; if exposed only to people they tend to become very 'humanised' despite the fact that they are later reared with other horses or ponies. This often produces an animal which is a pet that both expects and demands a great deal of attention; therefore, as far as possible foster mothers should be found for orphan foals. The National Foaling Bank (contact Miss Johanna Vardon, Meretown Stud, Salop; tel: (0952) 811234) gives assistance to anyone who has lost either a mare or a foal.

13: Mashes

A mash is made by adding boiling water or boiled food to bran. It has mildly laxative properties, so is often given before a day's rest, or to sick horses and those out of work; it also gives variety to the diet and is an ideal vehicle for worm medicines, feed supplements, etc.

The best-known form of mash is a bran mash, which is made in the following way:

You will need a bucket and one large or two smaller sacks (not paper bags) and a wooden stick.

About two-thirds fill the bucket with bran, according to the size of the horse or pony.

Mix in a small handful of salt.

Add boiling water and stir with the stick until all the bran is damp and the mixture is crumbly but not wet.

Cover with the sacks and leave it to cool down to blood-heat, when it will be ready to feed. The boiling water gradually cooks the bran. The length of time it takes to cool depends on the effectiveness of the insulation and the temperature of the day, but at least two to three hours should be allowed.

An alternative to the original bran mash is made by placing the horse's normal crushed oat and bran ration in a bucket and adding boiling water; in this case less water will be needed. The mixture should be well stirred and then covered with sacks, as described above. Where there is a large stable of horses, the mash is made in the feed barrow and the top of the barrow is covered over with sacks until feeding time.

Another type of mash in very common use, is made with linseed:

Linseed contains about 10 per cent mucilage which can only be digested by the micro-organisms in the large intestine; it is readily dispersed in water to form a jelly-like substance, which mixes well with bran. Linseed is high in protein and oil (see Chapter 6); the oil puts a shine on the horse's coat which becomes very apparent if it is fed linseed continuously every night for about three to four weeks, so this is used extensively when preparing animals for the show-ring or sales (See *Young Horse Management*).

Some linseed which has not been matured contains a cyanogenic glycoside and its associated enzyme linase, which together are capable of producing hydrogen cyanide. The enzyme is however destroyed by boiling, so to be on the safe side *all* linseed fed to horses should be boiled before feeding.

To make a linseed mash you will need one of the following items of equipment: a large saucepan, a domestic wash boiler or a special linseed boiler (see Chapter 1), and a cooker if a saucepan is used.

Buy whole linseed and use a single handful per horse.

Cover the linseed with cold water and leave it to soak overnight, bring to the boil in the morning and simmer gently until feeding time. If a saucepan is used, this can be covered and placed in a slow oven until required; the bottom oven of an Aga cooker is ideal. Linseed tends to boil over rather suddenly, so it must be watched very carefully while it is being brought to the boil.

To make the mash, add the linseed to the normal crushed oat and bran ration and mix well, then leave it to cool down to blood-heat before feeding.

Boiled feeds have an added advantage for the owner of a few horses, who does not own a grain crusher. Further variety can be obtained as certain food-stuffs, such as whole barley and field beans, can be bought direct from the farm at greatly reduced prices and boiled to make them digestible.

Cooking improves the digestibility of whole grain by 3 per cent. It ruptures the starch molecules as well as splitting the thick outer coat of the grain. It is a useful method of increasing the energy value of a ration, especially for horses which need to put on more weight. However, cooking speeds up the destruction of some vitamins by oxidation. It destroys any mould spores on the grain and slightly increases the length of time it takes for the 'cooked' protein to be absorbed, which can be an advantage.

Whole barley is commonly boiled with linseed; when mixed together there is less chance of their boiling over quite so suddenly, as with linseed on its own. It is usually fed at the rate of 1 part linseed:3—6 parts barley, but this should be adjusted according to the individual horse or pony.

As with a linseed mash, cover the grain with water and soak overnight; allow about twice as much water as for the linseed alone, since the barley grains swell considerably during cooking and therefore take up quite a lot of water. In the morning bring to the boil and boil for 10 minutes, then simmer for at least two hours. When cooked, the barley grains will split open and become quite soft. If insufficient water is allowed, the mixture will become one solid mass, so more should be added during the day if necessary.

Field beans are usually cracked before feeding but whole beans can be bought straight from the farm and boiled with the barley and linseed. They are very heating and should only be fed at the rate of a single handful per horse per day, but they provide a valuable source of protein. They should be boiled until they are quite soft, otherwise some horses will sort them out of their feed and leave them. In this case, where only a few horses are being fed, the beans can be squashed between the finger and thumb and mixed into the feed.

Broken-winded horses (see Chapter 11) and old horses whose teeth have worn smooth with age should be fed mashes rather than dry food.

Powdered additives should never be incorporated into a dry feed since the dust which they create can irritate the horse's lungs, which would at the very least make him cough.

Once a mash or damp feed has been made up, its keeping quality is very limited. Boiled barley, in particular, very soon starts to ferment if kept for more than a day, so mashes should only be made up as they are required and used the same day. Any feed left in a manger should be removed before the next feed is added and the manger cleaned out regularly. Damp food tends to collect on the sides of mangers much more quickly than dry food.

14: Horses at Grass

Grass is the natural food for horses and will potentially provide them with all the nutrients they require for maintenance (see graphs on page 122).

The management of grassland which is used specifically for horses requires considerably more attention than that which is used for other species of farm animal. Unlike these other animals which are usually herded together and driven into a building or yard en masse when required, the horse is caught up individually – therefore large paddocks are a distinct disadvantage. Small paddocks not exceeding six acres are to be recommended as on normal-sized stud farms these also enable the horses to be moved from one paddock to the next throughout the grazing season, thereby giving the horses a change of pasture and allowing the grass time to recover between grazings and also a percentage of the worm larvae time to die. To survive, all but the smallest pony needs an acre of good grassland for summer grazing or two acres for all-the-year-round use.

Horses are notoriously bad grazers – they tend to over-graze areas of their choice, leaving other parts of the paddock to grow away. They concentrate their droppings in specific areas over which they do not graze and this accentuates the pattern of rough coarse patches, surrounded by areas of over-grazed pasture. By nature horses tend to be creatures of habit – if allowed to remain in one particular paddock for any length of time, they will make permanent tracks in the sward. Most horses will gallop for fun or as a result of real or imagined fright, which, on heavy land or in wet weather, can result in strips of the sward being torn up and the pasture becoming badly poached, and these are ideal conditions for weeds to establish themselves and spread. Paddocks used exclusively or primarily for horses therefore need special and careful management if a good, healthy sward is to be maintained.

Where the acreage allows for mixed grazing, cattle should be grazed with the horses or, if preferred, follow them. This has the dual advantage of keeping the land evenly grazed and also reducing the incidence of worms, as well as avoiding a general unthriftiness which is commonly found where there is a high continuing concentration of any single species in a given area.

Where young horses and broodmares are concerned, it should be noted that only relatively mature non-lactating cattle should be used, as milking cows and calves tend to compete for the available minerals in the soil, which are depleted at the expense of the horses.

To get the best value from the grass, the land must be well drained and the soil in good condition — that is, there must not be any deficiency of lime, nitrogen, phosphate or potash. These minerals are all washed out of the top soil at differing rates over a period of time. Therefore regular soil analyses should be carried out — about once every three to five years — then any deficiency which becomes apparent can be corrected.

Calcium deficiency can lead to bone and joint troubles in young horses, as well as producing 'sour' grass. Depending on the soil and climatic conditions, an average loss of ground limestone per acre per year, due to leaching and plant growth, is in the region of four units.

Nitrogen directly affects the yield of grass and is supplied in three ways:
1. From the droppings and urine of the grazing animals;

2. The clover in the sward — this will usually contribute between 100 and 200 units per acre of nitrogen per season;

3. From the manure or fertiliser applied to the land.

Horses and ponies are not usually kept in very great concentration on a paddock, as compared with cattle. In many cases their droppings are removed, so there is less likelihood of a satisfactory build-up of nitrogen in the soil from this source. Applications of farmyard manure, at the rate of twelve tonnes to the acre, each autumn — not poultry manure which is too high in nitrogen — will supply the following amounts of available plant nutrients during the season of application, thereby reducing the amount of other fertilisers needed:

N	P_2O_5	K_2O
33 units	40 units	90 units
(17 kg)	(20 kg)	(46 kg)

Organic fertilisers are released at a slower rate than artificial fertilisers, and therefore do not produce the rapid growth of grass which can produce both leg and digestive troubles in horses.

Phosphates are essential for good root development in the plants, and therefore benefit the growth of clover, which in turn helps the nitrogen level. A maintenance dressing in the region of 75—100 units of phosphate per acre every three years is usually recommended for grazing land, but higher dressings should be applied when paddocks are being re-seeded. Soil analysis ensures that fertilisers are used to best advantage.

Potash is necessary for healthy plants; on normal land, deficiencies usually occur only when high rates of nitrogen are applied, and the grass is mown or very heavily grazed, in which case fifty units of K_2O may be necessary. An annual dressing of half this amount should be sufficient for most horse paddocks.

Horses are very selective grazers. Therefore palatibility

is of great importance and strains of grass should be selected with this in mind. Nearly all grasses are palatable when young, but some become less palatable with age. Leafy varieties have a higher protein content, with lower fibre, and are therefore more digestible. Cocksfoot, except when very young, is too coarse and tends to be rejected by horses. Soil types and local climatic conditions will influence the actual varieties and quantities of each used in a paddock mixture; your local A.D.A.S. (Agricultural Development Advisory Service) officer in England and Wales should be consulted when in doubt.

Since horses have the habit of cropping areas of their paddock down to ground level, care should be taken not to include too much clover in a mixture, as under heavy grazing conditions this will tend to grow away at the expense of the grass – providing a lower over-all yield of herbage per acre. A mixture containing several different varieties of grass, as well as herbs and clover, is ideal for horses.

Paddock grasses must be able to withstand poaching to a high degree. Therefore they must have good tillering ability – that is, the ability to give off new shoots at their base and thus spread out at ground level. Grasses which exhibit speed of recovery after grazing are also very desirable.

In the early spring the paddocks should be harrowed, to pull out the dead grass and spread any remaining manure. After harrowing, the paddocks should be rolled with a heavy flat grass roller – the Cambridge type is too light for most grassland. Throughout the spring, summer and autumn, when the land is not too wet, the paddocks should be topped, chain harrowed and rolled between grazings. Harrowing and rolling, in particular, should be carried out slowly for maximum efficiency. Topping is absolutely essential when mixed grazing is not practised, to maintain an even growth rate of the grass right across the paddock together with the maximum nutritional value and palatability.

Horses and ponies may be kept at grass without any supplementary feeding, if the following conditions hold good:

1. There is a sufficient quantity of palatable grass available;

2. The quality of the grass is high enough to provide maintenance at the very least;

3. The horse or pony in question is not in hard work.

With reference to the graphs in Fig. 26, it can be seen that the rate of growth varies enormously throughout the year. In some areas, particularly the Eastern counties of England, the grass burns up completely during July and when this happens supplementary feeding is essential to maintain the animals' condition. The September flush usually provides a good bite but by then most of the goodness has gone out of the grass; that is, it has a lower soluble carbohydrate and protein and higher fibre percentage than spring grass. During the winter months there is virtually no growth at all, so supplementary feeding must be practised. Other factors which influence the nutritive value of grass include the brightness or dullness of the day — the soluble carbohydrate content is higher on sunny days. Rainfall can affect the mineral composition — calcium tends to be present in the plants in higher amounts during drought periods and phosphorus levels rise when rainfall is high.

A good horseman constantly watches both the amount and quality of grass available on his paddocks and equates this with the condition of the horses. No hard and fast rules can ever be laid down and the decision when to supplement the grass can only be made by the individual himself.

A constant supply of clean fresh water must be available at all times.

ENGLAND

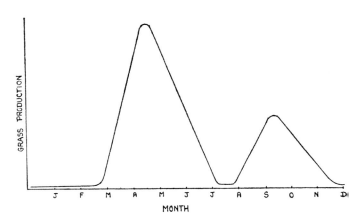

IRELAND

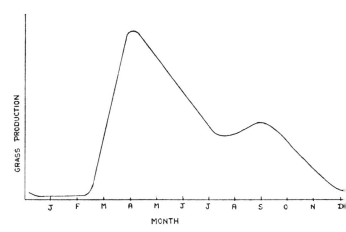

Fig. 26 Graphs showing average monthly grass production for England and Ireland. The low trough between July and August on the graph for England is due to drought periods – more often seen in eastern areas of the country

When horses are kept out all the year round, extra food will be necessary during cold weather, especially when it is both cold and wet, so that the horse can compensate for the cooling effect of the wind and/or rain. Most horses will stand cold dry weather fairly well but when it is both cold and wet, all but hardy native ponies should be offered some form of shelter.

The moment the quality or quantity of the grass declines, supplementary feeding must be given. The easiest way to do this outside is to feed hay and nuts. The hay can be placed in hay racks or it can be dropped off in piles across the field, always allowing between one and three more piles of hay than there are horses or ponies in the field, depending on the exact number, to prevent fighting. Choose the cleanest and most sheltered areas, giving sufficient room between the various piles and the nearest fence or hedge so that bullied animals do not find themselves trapped. Allow about one 40-lb bale of hay between every two to four animals according to their size and the value of the grass. Nuts may also be placed in piles in just the same way as the hay, or they should be placed in troughs in the middle of the paddock or on the fence. One trough per horse should be allowed and the troughs must be placed 50 feet apart to prevent fighting.

Alternatively, if a field shelter is available the hay and food can be placed in this, which is of course a big advantage if the weather is wet, but no animal which is a bully should be left in the paddock.

15: Feeding Stabled Horses

The stabled horse or pony has to rely one hundred per cent on the people who are looking after him to provide all his needs — nutritional and otherwise. Therefore anyone who looks after a stabled horse owes it to that horse to acquire a working knowledge of the subject of stable management and feeding.

Horses always do best if a regular routine, with regular feeding times, is established, as this gives them the greatest peace of mind, but it can be worked out to suit both the horses and their owner. The great thing is to try to ensure that horses and ponies are given their feeds at a time when there is a complete absence of human activity in the yard; this means that the horses will be able to concentrate on eating their food rather than thinking about other things. Happy, contented horses thrive best.

Most people divide the daily ration into two to four feeds, making the last one the largest of the day, as the horse then has the most time to eat and digest his food. Ideally the feeds should be as evenly spaced out as possible, so most people feed at the following times:

7.30 am   12.30 pm   5.00 pm   10.00 pm

although any other group of times is likely to be equally satisfactory, if they fit into a particular routine better than those given above; horses soon get used to receiving their first feed at 10 am and their last feed at midnight if necessary.

Usually the first time you see your horses in the morning is when you take the feed in to them, therefore the natural reaction of most people is to check that the night feed has been cleaned up and to remove any uneaten food before placing the morning feed in the manger, and to stand back and examine the horse. Instinct will usually tell you if anytthing is wrong the moment you enter the box but a minute or two spent looking at the horse will not be time wasted; observe how he tucks into his food, look carefully at his condition and note if there is any alteration for better or worse and work out in your mind how you can encourage or rectify the change by altering the diet slightly. If you have a broodmare with a foal at foot, always remember to check that the mare's udder is empty each morning, especially before you turn them out – a filled udder usually means that the foal is 'off suck' and therefore probably feeling ill. Also remember to check that the horse's droppings are of the right consistency, i.e. not too soft or particularly not too hard.

If a horse fails to clean up a feed, remove the old food from the manger preferably at least one hour before you give him his next feed and this feed should be reduced slightly in quantity, to encourage the horse to eat up. It often pays to miss one feed out altogether once a week, as this gives the digestive system a rest and often makes the horse keener. A well-balanced ration is even more important for stabled horses than for those with access to good grazing, as they must receive an adequate supply of amino acids, starch, fibre, vitamins and minerals to satisfy their needs.

Protein is necessary even for adult horses and ponies, as it is used for the repair and replacement of tissue, a continuous process in both young and old alike. No adjustment to the protein level of their rations is necessary, since these animals receive higher grain rations with increasing work which automatically increases the quantity of protein fed. Young horses, broodmares in the last third of their gestation, and during lactation, require increased levels of protein. Protein is composed of amino acids and these must be supplied in a balanced form in the feed, otherwise an amino-acid deficiency may occur and then the horse will not 'do' as well.

Energy is supplied from the breakdown of carbohydrate, either in the form of starch or fibre. Foals and horses in hard work require a high starch/low fibre diet. A high fibre diet of necessity allows a large percentage of undigested food to reach the hind gut, the mechanical effect of which is undesirable in horses doing fast work. The horse's metabolism can utilise the energy produced from starch more efficiently than it can the volatile fatty acids which are produced from the breakdown of fibre. The young foal has not developed a full microbial digestion so it cannot deal effectively with a high fibre diet. Store horses and animals doing slow work can be given diets which are higher in fibre. The horse's condition is therefore governed by the amount of starch and digestible fibre in his diet.

Stabled horses usually appreciate something succulent as an addition to their diet. New tastes should be introduced in very small quantities, allowing the horse plenty of time to get used to the flavour before he is given a normal quantity. Succulent foods normally include:

Carrots — these should be fed whole or chopped lengthways, to prevent any chance of choking. Misshaped carrots can usually be bought quite cheaply direct from growers. Unwashed carrots keep the best; once they have been washed their keeping time is reduced to less than a week.

Apples — should also be chopped to prevent choking.

Turnips — some horses and ponies will eat these and once they have acquired a taste for them, some will take a delight in gnawing their way through a whole turnip.

Grass or lucerne — a patch of lucerne can be especially grown and cut as required for stabled horses, or a patch of grass can be saved for the same purpose; both are equally well appreciated.

Care must, however, be taken when giving succulents to horses and ponies, as excess amounts or even otherwise normal quantities, when given to horses which are not used to them, can cause scouring and limit intake of other foodstuffs.

Stabled horses mostly have a higher vitamin requirement than horses which are turned out, particularly in the case of vitamins A and D. Vitamins are available from:
1. The foodstuffs;
2. Microbial synthesis in the gut — B vitamins;
3. Synthesis within the tissues — vitamin D;
4. Maternal transfer through the uterus to the foetus.
Vitamins are dealt with in detail in Chapter 2.

Minerals are required in different amounts by different horses; the main factors which affect this requirement are:
1. The body weight of the horse;
2. Growth rate — the faster the growth rate the more minerals are required;
3. Type of animal — broodmares which are lactating require more minerals;
4. Horses which sweat a lot also have a higher demand;
5. The age of the animal — younger horses absorb minerals better than older horses;
6. The individual element—some are more easily absorbed than others;
7. The general health of the animal;
8. The presence of essential substances for absorption — calcium requires vitamin D.

Most of the minerals are absorbed from various parts of the small intestine; any excess is voided in the faeces, and any excess which has already been absorbed is got rid of in the urine.

Stabled horses must be supplied with salt licks and should at least be given a calcium supplement to balance the high phosphorus levels of a normal grain diet.

Horses are capable of storing higher levels of vitamin A in their livers than most other farm animals but if they are not allowed access to green grass for several months then a deficiency may occur. Similarly vitamin D, which is formed from the action of sunlight on the horse's skin, may be deficient when horses are stabled throughout the summer months; it may also be deficient in all horses during the winter months.

Most stabled horses and ponies on normal diets, should be given an *ad lib* supply of good hay. This should be offered to them after exercise and exercise should not be given until at least an hour after a feed. The only horses and ponies which need not be given hay are those on complete nuts — where this is recommended (see Chapter 11).

As with all animals and man, horses have a limited daily capacity for food which varies with individuals even of the same size, but is normally taken to be in the region of 2.5 per cent of body weight, varying from approximately 18 lb for small ponies to as much as twice this amount for large horses. One can therefore either give the horse his entire ration in the form of good hay or allow so much corn and make the rest up with hay. Good hay will supply all the nutrients needed by a horse or pony which is not in work, but once an animal is required to do any work he will need an extra supply of energy and protein to maintain his condition. If horses are to be kept on hay alone, their condition must be watched very carefully, as the value of the hay determines whether it will be capable of supplying maintenance or whether a supplement will also be necessary and this can vary between individual horses.

It is normal practice in most stables to give a definite

quantity (or weight) of corn each day and allow the horse to make up the deficiency in his bulk requirement with hay; obviously the more corn he receives the less hay he will want to eat.

The following quantities of a straight ration of nuts are given as a rough guide but they must be adjusted according to the individual animal's requirements, i.e. the amount of work he is doing and his condition. No two horses or ponies ever give exactly the same response to any given diet — this is the reason why horses must always be fed as individuals and not as a group, if their maximum potential is to be achieved.

Ponies up to 12.2 hands   3 — 9 lb feed/day
Ponies from 12.2 – 14.2 hands   9 – 12 lb feed/day
Horses from 14.2 – 16.2 hands   12 – 16 lb feed/day

Many people keep horses and ponies which they ride for a short time in the evenings or at week-ends. Their main problem is usually how to maintain the horse's condition without letting him get too fresh.

The following foodstuffs are suitable for this purpose:

Dried grass meal or nuts — soaked overnight;

Bran — but it must be well supplemented with calcium otherwise deficiency symptoms will occur;

Sugar-beet pulp or nuts — must be soaked for 24 hours before feeding, otherwise it can cause colic. It does help to balance the calcium:phosphorus ratio when fed in conjunction with bran, but as the protein is of such poor quality a protein supplement is still necessary for broodmares and young stock;

Flaked maize — high energy, low calcium, therefore a calcium supplement is essential.

About ½ lb of a protein food, such as soya bean meal, milk powder or some grain balancer nuts, should be added to improve the protein level of the diet for mares and foals.

Calcium can be supplied in the form of ground limestone or as calcium lactate.

Horses in medium work will do well on a mixture of
1 part bran;
1 part grass meal;
6 parts oats;
plus protein and calcium supplements as above.

Horses on hard work should be given clipped oats to reduce the fibre intake as much as possible; bran should only be given in moderation, as this too is high in fibre. Only the best quality hay should be given. Horses in hard work have a higher level of muscular wear and tear than other horses, therefore they require a slightly higher level of protein in their diets and this is even more important if the horses are also still growing. In these cases up to 15 per cent soya bean meal may be added to their diet each day.

All stabled horses should receive a mash every night, as this adds variety to the diet and helps to keep up the horse's appetite, apart from providing a vehicle for worm medicines. Linseed will help to keep their coats looking well.

A good barometer of an individual's response to his diet is the condition of his droppings. Ideally these should just break up as they reach the ground. If they are too wet or too dry and hard, the diet and/or exercise should be altered accordingly. Under-exercise tends to cause constipation in stabled horses, therefore horses which are standing without exercise for a day or longer should have their food reduced accordingly and be given mashes, otherwise they could develop colic. Damp bran is a well-known laxative.

Horses with loose droppings can be tightened up if they are given feeds containing dry bran. High-protein diets and new hay can cause loose droppings;

in the former case reduce the protein level until the droppings return to normal.

Not all cases of loose droppings are due to nutritional errors, therefore the horse's temperature should be checked and a veterinary surgeon called if necessary, and also where the condition does not respond to an alteration in the diet. This is particularly important in the case of foals, who tend to suffer from diarrhoea at some time in their lives before weaning, and if neglected they can die.

16: Feeding Broodmares and Young Horses

The developing foetus makes little, if any, demand on the mare's metabolism until the last third of the gestation period, then the protein level of the diet should be increased to approximately 11 per cent to counteract the increasing demand of the unborn foal. The effect of spring grass on the birth weights of foals from mares receiving a traditional diet, but turned out each day, can be clearly seen from Fig. 27.

Once the mare has foaled, the protein level of her diet should be increased still further to about 14 per cent, to enable her to give the maximum milk yield of which she is capable. This is very important because the growth rate of the unweaned foal is closely related to its mother's environment as well as its own, and one of the most influential factors is the availability of food. Other factors which have a bearing on the growth rate include:

Environmental temperature;

Inherited factors;

Social stress – e.g. overcrowding.

At first there is a rapid increase in the size of the foal, which gradually slows down until the animal reaches an adult state, when no more growth takes place; this is usually at or about three years of age. The bones grow at the fastest rate, followed by muscle tissue and then fat; skeletal growth can only take place so long as the epiphyseal plates remain open – closure takes place at varying times for the different bones, i.e. the epiphyses above the fetlock joints usually close at about nine

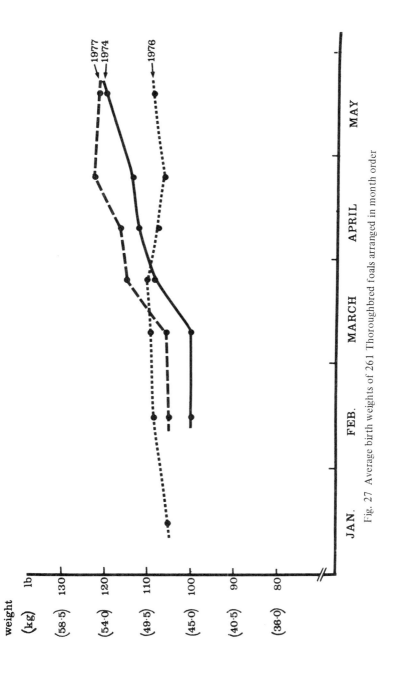

weight

(kg) lb

Fig. 27 Average birth weights of 261 Thoroughbred foals arranged in month order

months of age and those above the knee at about eighteen months to two and a half years.

Growth is affected by such factors as:

Nutrition   Environment
Genetics   Exercise and work
Appetite and repletion   Parasites
Disease   Reproduction
Hormones

The long bones grow in length from the epiphyseal plates which are located near their ends; they increase in size from the periosteum (skin covering the bone). Colts tend to have more bone than fillies; size of bone is partly an inherited characteristic and partly due to nutrition but large bones are not always synonymous with density and strength.

Both heredity and environment influence the growth of the individual horse or pony. Apart from nutrition the next most important factor relating to environment is the weather. The temperature, humidity, wind, amount of sun, rain, snow and above all the rate of change in the weather all have a large effect on the growth rate.

Food can be wasted in cold weather if adequate shelter is not provided for horses; this can lead to a reduced growth rate in young horses. Horses produce body heat as a waste product of metabolism (see diagram on page 87). To maintain an even temperature this body heat is lost at exactly the rate of production, but if the atmospheric temperature drops then the horse must produce more heat to prevent its body temperature from falling and this process uses up valuable energy from the food. As the animal grows, so its heat production and insulation increases, therefore great care must be taken not to expose very young foals to cold, wet weather. Voluntary food intake is affected by temperature; more food tends to be eaten in cold weather and less when the weather is hot. Food intake is also regulated by such factors as distension of the stomach, and the amount of energy the food contains.

Proper feeding provides a balanced supply of energy, protein, lipids, vitamins and minerals and these supply the essentials for normal growth. Growth is also affected by hormones; the reader will probably have noticed that there is usually a fairly level rate of growth in both sexes up to the time of sexual maturity, then the male sex hormone (testosterone) produces a reduction in the rate of closure of the colts' epiphyses, allowing growth to continue unchecked at this time. Oestrogens, the female sex hormones, on the other hand, help to promote epiphyseal closure and   therefore slow down the growth rate in fillies. Testosterone also helps to develop the masculine characteristics and produces a greater muscle growth.

Some plants contain naturally occurring oestrogens and these should not be given in quantity to broodmares. They do, however, produce surprising positive growth responses when fed to young horses of both sexes. The two most common feeds which contain oestrogens are lucerne (Alfalfa) and soya bean meal.

Growth responses are often observed after administering worm medicines (anthelmintics) but these are more than likely due to the fact that parasites have been eliminated from the gut, rather than to the effect of the drug itself on the growth rate. If it is suspected that any young horses or ponies have worms, care should be taken not to push them too hard immediately after worming, as the sudden surge in growth rate can only too easily result in epiphysitis (see page 102). Ideally all youngstock should be wormed every month to prevent any build-up of parasitic infection, using for example a Mebendazole (Telmin) syringe one month and a Pyrantel embonate (Strongid) syringe the next, to prevent the parasites becoming immune to the effects of any one particular drug. Many authorities now recommend the use of ivermectin (Eqvalan).

When feeding young horses, one of the most important facts to bear in mind is that until they are about seven months old they have not developed a full adult microbial digestion system in their large intestine and should therefore be given only high-quality foods, particularly good-class hay, up to this time.

A foal will not consume very much solid food for the first few weeks of its life, but will rely on its mother's milk, the quanitity and quality of which will be largely determined by her diet as well as by inherited factors governing milk yield. During this period of maximum growth it has been estimated that the foal requires just over ½ lb of digestible protein for every 1 lb gain in body weight, which is initially supplied by the milk alone.

The young foal should be given every encouragement to eat: for this reason, wherever possible, long mangers should be constructed in loose-boxes used for mares with foals at foot and these should be built about 2 ft 6 in. (75 cm) from the ground, so that even young foals can reach into them quite easily. (See diagram on page 16.) The food should be scattered along the full length of the trough to help prevent too much free competition from the mare. As the foal gets older and it becomes more important that he really does get his share of food, 'bossy' mares should be tied up while the foal eats. When mares and foals are running at grass, the situation can be quite easily dealt with by building a creep-feed system. A square fence is built round one or more feed troughs. The fence is made just high enough so that the foals can walk underneath, but not high enough to let any mares through. The posts should be placed nearer together than usual to afford extra strength. An alternative method is to build narrow openings in the fence sides, just wide enough for the foals but too narrow for the mares to squeeze through. Most foals do particularly well when reared outside all the time from about two months old onwards and once the warmer spring weather comes. However, breeders should realise that the mare's nutrient requirements are high, at least until three to four months of lactation. Mares receiving no supplementary feed at this time are likely to lose weight unless they have access to plenty of good grass. Therefore it is better if mares and foals are brought into their looseboxes for a feed each day. This also allows the foal to become accustomed to being handled.

Part of the art of feeding young horses is to think of spring grass as the ideal food and then balance the ration according to the value of the grass available. When there is plenty of spring grass about no extra feed is really necessary, but as the value of the grass declines through the year so extra food must be given to maintain an even growth rate. The annual rate of grass production in England and Ireland is shown on page 122. It should be noted that the 'autumn flush' of grass is lower in protein and higher in fibre than spring grass.

Most young horses appreciate a mash as an alternative to their normal nut or oat, bran and balancer ration. Money can be saved by buying whole grain, etc., direct from the farm and boiling it until soft. These can be fed at the rate of:

<pre>
½ lb whole barley   ⎫
2 oz field beans   ⎬ per horse per day
1 oz whole linseed ⎭
</pre>

Mix this with one part bran to six parts oats, the quantity used being adjusted to the individual horse's requirements. To increase the protein level of this ration, soya bean meal may be added at the rate of 5 oz per day for foals, or 1 lb per day for horses over a year old, having been increased gradually over a period of time. Alternatively about the same quantity of milk powder may be used.

Grass meal can be used as a protein supplement for horses over two years. It is a very fine powder; the easiest way to deal with this is to soak it in water before mixing with the oats. However, do not use too much water otherwise the result will be a wet feed. Grass nuts are not accepted by some horses; when this is the case, they can be broken down to a meal by soaking them in a little water overnight. When lucerne meal is used in conjunction with oats and no bran is fed, there is no need to add any calcium to the ration, but in all other cases about 1 oz or more of ground limestone should be used.

The calcium:phosphorus ratio is very important as far as growing horses are concerned and also in the case of lactating mares and those in the last four months of their pregnancy. A quick glance at the chart on page 157 will reveal that most of the grain we feed our horses is deficient in calcium and since the ratio should not be allowed to fall below 1.1:1, a daily calcium supplement is essential. The two most readily absorbed forms of calcium are calcium lactate and calcium gluconate.

All foals should be well established on their diet *before* weaning and this diet should be maintained exactly *after* weaning, to avoid any check in the foal's growth rate. Where more than one mare and foal is kept, paddock weaning is to be recommended (see *Young Horse Management*). Foals must receive highly nourishing feeds at this time; should a foal go off his food during weaning, he must be brought back to his full ration very gradually over a period of time, otherwise there will be a sudden surge in the growth rate which almost inevitably leads to 'round joints'.

Pregnant mares in the last ninety days of gestation and during lactation, as well as all young horses up to twenty-four months old, must have a source of high-quality protein in their diet. The mare's requirement for nutrients is higher *after* foaling than before. Rations should be constructed to include one of the following quality protein foods:

Extracted or full fat soya bean meal

Skimmed milk powder

High-grade white fish meal

In all cases the calcium:phosphorus ratio must be adjusted to bring the available calcium higher than the available phosphorus. For this reason it is usually better to aim for a 1.5:1 ratio for broodmares and youngstock.

Since over-fat young horses are most prone to epiphysitis no young horse should be overfed. Sounder animals are produced when their growth rate is not forced.

17: Feeding Compound Nuts or Cubes

Nuts and cubes, as used for horse feeding, are generally made up from a scientifically balanced ration, which has first been ground to a uniform powdered consistency and then compressed to form nuts or cubes – which are just different names for the same product. Contrary to popular belief nuts are not a very new idea, as they were used by the Russian and German armies during World War II, and in some private stables before that time.

Briefly, all large manufacturers of animal feeds buy their ingredients in bulk, which enables them to obtain the best-quality foodstuffs available at the right price in both the home and world markets.

Most of these manufacturers produce a very comprehensive range of cubed feeds for all types and ages of horse or pony, catering for everything from the foal through to its emergence as a racehorse, hunter, riding horse, broodmare, etc. The national compounders and some local compounders employ scientists and formulation experts, to work out the very best rations possible. Many of the larger ones carry out research into all aspects of equine nutrition and so constantly strive to better their feeds and consequently also the health and performance of the animals to which they are fed. The research work carried out in the laboratories is backed up by trials with horses, which ensures that every ration formulated is palatable and that none of the ingredients it contains has any undesirable side-effects. From time to time the quality or availability of certain ingredients alters and then the whole ration may have to be reformulated. To eliminate any chance of error, computers are used by the larger firms to process the information to hand and control the flow of ingredients from the blender bins through the automatic weighing system into the mixers.

Before the various ingredients can be made up into nuts or cubes they must be thoroughly ground and blended. To achieve this, they are passed through a hammer mill before being mixed together. As a pre-caution the hammer mills are fitted with magnets which remove any stray metal particles before the ingredients enter the grinding chamber. As they are ground, the particles of food are drawn by suction through a metal screen into a chamber where they are usually treated with dry steam and/or some molasses are added to aid pelleting; the mixture is then well agitated and passed through a press.

The press works on a similar principle to an ordinary kitchen meat grinder, in as much as it is fitted with vertical revolving plates in which holes of a predetermined size have been drilled. The meal is forced through the holes by compression, and a set of knives on the outside cut the cubes to any given length.

At this stage the cubes are still soft and hot so they are passed through a cooling chamber, which is venti-lated by means of suction fans. Here they are cooled as quickly as possible and any dust particles are removed from the hardened nuts before packaging.

In the larger mills routine tests are carried out by the laboratory technicians at all stages in the process, from the time the raw materials are being purchased to the point when the final product leaves the factory; this system helps to ensure uniform quality at all times.

The following range of feeds is usually available:
1. A low protein (10 per cent)/relatively high fibre

(15 per cent) nut, suitable for feeding with hay, to horses and ponies in light work;

2. A higher protein (14 per cent)/low fibre (9 per cent) nut, for horses in hard work;

3. A relatively high protein (15 per cent)/low fibre (5 per cent) nut, for young growing horses and ponies, which is also suitable for broodmares in the last one-third of their gestation;

4. A low protein (10 per cent)/high fibre (20 per cent) nut, formulated to supply the total needs of horses in ordinary work and given with little or no hay. Where horses are in hard work, a higher protein/low fibre nut should also be included in the ration;

5. A grain balancer nut – for people who grow their own oats or prefer to feed oats with their nuts; these simply help to balance the traditional oat and hay ration.

Some people prefer to make up their own rations for horses, either because over the years they have achieved very satisfactory results, probably producing animals which have been in better condition or performed better than their neighbours', or because they feel that this is part of the fun of keeping horses and would not consider changing to anything else, while others swear by cube feeding. There are several advantages and disadvantages for both systems which can probably be summed up as follows:

The main argument which is usually put forward against cube feeding is that the user cannot see the individual ingredients in the nuts and must therefore rely on the manufacturer for their quality and formulation. It is therefore absolutely essential that nuts are bought from reputable compounders.

Nuts take all the fun out of feeding horses and cubed rations are only as flexible as the range of feeds made available by the manufacturers, as the addition of any single ingredient by the feeder will tend to unbalance the whole ration.

Complete nuts — those which include the hay ration — can create boredom, which in turn tends to produce stable vices such as crib-biting, windsucking and wood-chewing. This is due to the fact that the horse eats his food and then because adequate roughage has been included in the ration and no hay is fed, the horse has nothing to occupy his mind and soon invents his own entertainment.

There is no room for the traditional twice-weekly mash in a wholly cube-feeding programme, and a further major disadvantage is that it is virtually impossible to include any medicines in a cube ration.

Horses on cube rations drink more water than those on a traditional diet.

Against the foregoing disadvantages, cubes are an absolute godsend to anyone with limited storage space. Where horses are kept in suburban areas which afford little or no room for the storage of hay or many bags containing different types of foodstuff, complete cubes are probably the only answer. For the same reason cubes are the answer when horses are being transported over long distances, especially by road or sea.

Not all ingredients with a high dietary value are very palatable to all horses, and if included in a straight ration some would be sorted out and rejected; however, when included in nuts they are automatically accepted without any trouble. For the same reason there is no wastage of food when horses are given cubes at the recommended levels, as the manufacturers ensure a high degree of palatability.

Due to the methods employed in the manufacture of the cubes, all mould spores are destroyed (however, it should be borne in mind that toxins produced by any moulds may still remain) and dust is virtually eliminated; in consequence there is less risk of coughing and broken wind (see Chapter 11).

When complete nuts are fed, all 'hay-bellies' disappear as there is no great bulk of fibre in the hind gut.

Horses are capable of eating a greater weight of nuts than of a traditional ration, due to the more rapid passage of the ground food through the digestive tract; this can be of significance for horses with poor appetites.

The droppings of horses fed on nothing but cubes are maintained at the correct consistency all the time.

Due to the fact that the ingredients have already been well ground-up, cubes, unless they are very hard, are easier for older horses to both chew and digest.

Cubes have the added advantage that they adapt readily to automatic feeding devices and are especially useful where foals are being creep-fed (see Fig. 28).

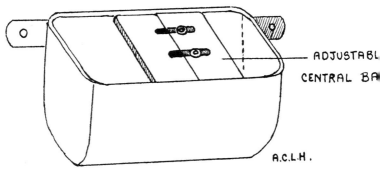

ADJUSTABL

CENTRAL BA

A.C.L.H .

Fig. 28 Metal creep-feeder for unweaned foals enables a foal to eat without competition from its dam. Available from Horse Requisites, Newmarket, Suffolk

Cubes are also the method of choice when it comes to feeding large numbers of horses running out together in a paddock, especially when the food is dropped off in small piles on the ground. This way there is little, if any, wastage.

When a traditional straight ration is given, the feeder

has to be able to judge the quality of the various samples of oats, hay, etc., as they come into the yard and must be prepared to adjust the rations accordingly — that is, literally from one delivery to the next. By using cubes, consistent quality is assured, as any quality adjustment has already been carried out by the manufacturer.

As the cube ration has already been scientifically balanced and formulated, there is no great mystique attached to this method of feeding, so even someone without any prior knowledge of feeding can distribute the nuts, so long as they follow the manufacturers' instructions which come with every bag. Under the traditional system a stable can be in trouble if the regular feeder is taken ill suddenly or has an accident and nobody else knows exactly what the horses have been receiving.

Lastly, cubes are generally marketed in 25 kilos (56 lb) bags which is a convenient size for most people to handle.

Appendix—Analysis of Foodstuffs

NUTRITIONAL AVAILABILITY OF FOODSTUFFS

All foodstuffs can be broken down into two distinct parts: the indigestible organic matter (IOM), which is not available to the horse; and the total digestible nutrients (TDN) which are available to the horse. The latter can be further broken down into the following categories:

(i)   The percentage protein and its amino acid composition;
(ii) The digestible energy of the various foods;
(iii) Their fibre content;
(iv) Their vitamin and mineral content including the calcium:phosphorus ratio of the foods.

This information has been included as a reference, so that readers can construct better balanced rations for their horses or ponies using these charts as a guide.

The figures given should be taken as an indication of the average composition of each food; since all these foods are derived from growing matter, it should be borne in mind that there is bound to be a slight variation between samples, depending on where and how they were grown and the weather conditions prevailing during growth and harvest.

The good feeder tries to buy the best samples available and should always bear in mind the area in which the crop was grown, e.g. oats grown in Scotland and dried grass from Ireland are usually considered better than the same product grown in other areas of the British Isles in most seasons.

Most of the data for the charts which appear on the following pages are 'Crown Copyright' – reproduced from MAFF ADAS Advisory Paper No. 11 (2nd edition, 1976).

Low values are desirable

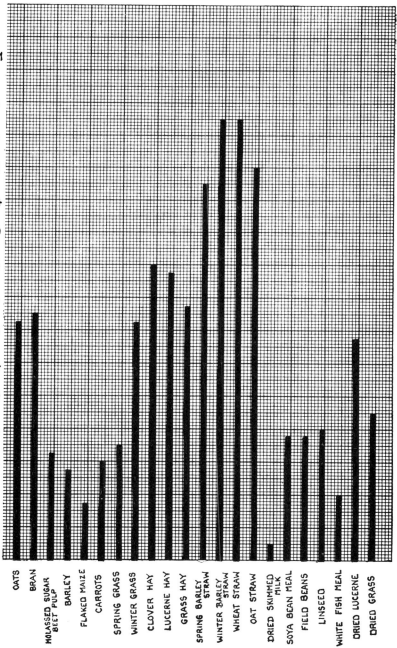

PROTEIN

Protein is made up from a number of different amino acids which are present in the individual foodstuffs in characteristic proportions.

All farm foods contain protein as well as energy, vitamins and minerals. Proportions vary; concentrate foods containing more than 35 per cent protein are high-protein; those with 20 to 35 per cent are medium-protein; and those with less than 20 per cent are low-protein. Low-protein foods, such as those shown on page 149, make up the largest part of any mix.

Mature horses which are not under stress have no critical requirement for protein quality (i.e. amino acid composition) but youngstock up to 24 months old and broodmares in the last 90 days of gestation and during lactation do. The latter must have their diets supplemented with a high-grade protein such as extracted or full-fat soya bean meal, fish meal or skimmed milk powder.

Protein is measured in terms of percentage crude protein (CP) or digestible protein (DP) – which is the amount of dietary protein digested by the horse.

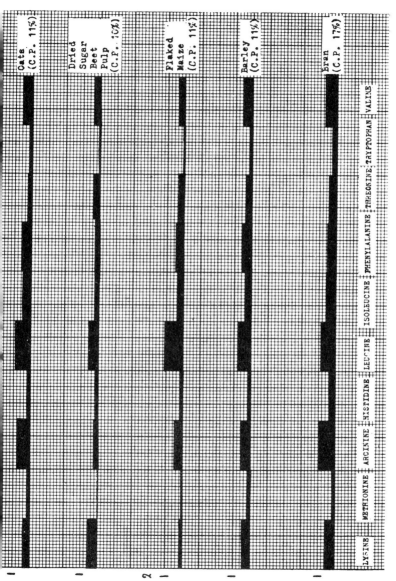

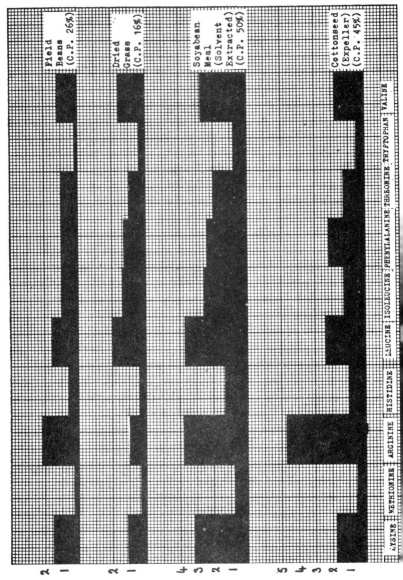

% in food

Field Beans (C.P. 26%)

Dried Grass (C.P. 16%)

Soyabean Meal (Solvent Extracted) (C.P. 50%)

Cottonseed (Expeller) (C.P. 45%)

LYSINE METHIONINE ARGININE HISTIDINE LEUCINE ISOLEUCINE PHENYLALANINE THREONINE TRYPTOPHAN VALINE

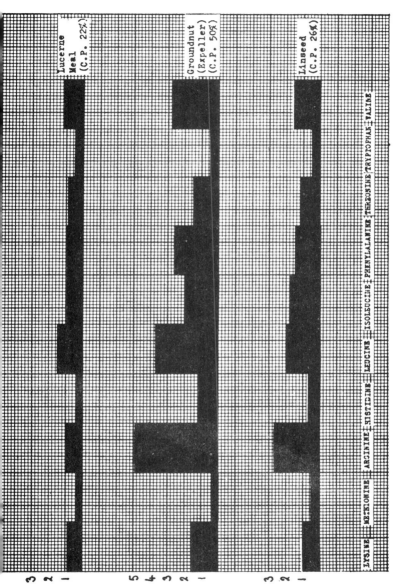

% in food

LYSINE METHIONINE ARGININE HISTIDINE LEUCINE ISOLEUCINE PHENYLALANINE THREONINE TRYPTOPHAN VALINE

Lucerne Meal (C.P. 22%)

Groundnut (Expeller) (C.P. 50%)

Linseed (C.P. 26%)

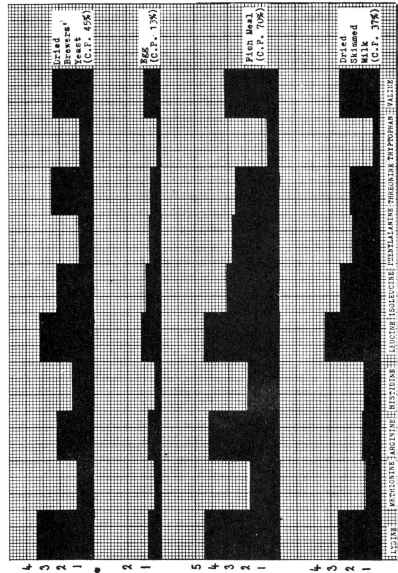

% in food

LYSINE · METHIONINE · ARGININE · HISTIDINE · LEUCINE · ISOLEUCINE · PHENYLALANINE · THREONINE · TRYPTOPHAN · VALINE

Dried Brewers' Yeast (C.P. 45%)

Egg (C.P. 13%)

Fish Meal (C.P. 70%)

Dried Skimmed Milk (C.P. 37%)

DIGESTIBLE ENERGY

The horse's nutritional requirements for energy are met by glucose (mostly from grain) and fatty acids (from the breakdown of fibre in the large intestine) as well as from fats and excess protein in the diet.

Food energy is commonly measured in megajoules per kilogramme (MJ/kg).

The chart on page 154 gives an indication of the total energy value of some more common foodstuffs and page 155 shows which of these are high in fibre energy and therefore to be avoided or given only in moderation when feeding foals or horses in hard work.

Dietary energy governs the horse's condition (i.e. whether he is fat or thin).

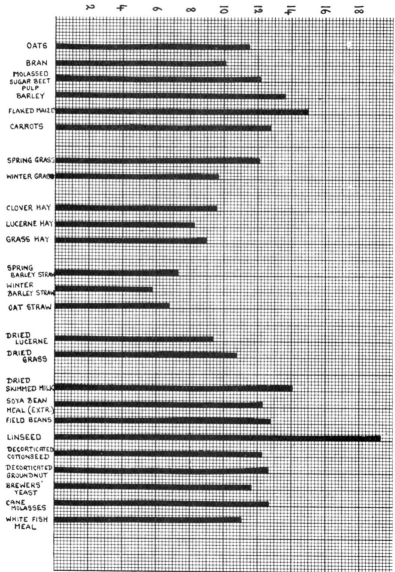

MJ/kg.

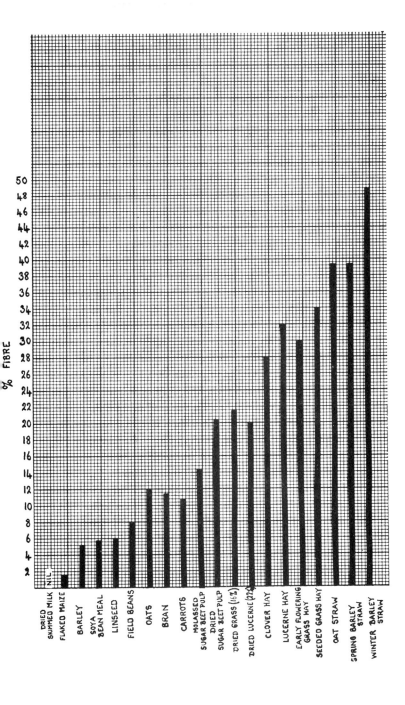

% FIBRE

CALCIUM AND PHOSPHORUS

The calcium:phosphorus ratio is important for all horses, and an imbalance can create problems even in adult horses but it is vital for young horses and brood-mares in the last third of gestation and during lactation.

The ratio should never fall below 1.1:1.

A quick glance at the chart on page 157 will reveal that most of the more common foodstuffs we give our horses are deficient in calcium, particularly bran which also contains high levels of phosphorus. Therefore some form of calcium supplement should be given every day.

The absorption of calcium is closely linked with the availability of vitamin D (the sunlight vitamin), therefore this too should be supplemented in the case of stabled horses and others during the winter and early spring months, as there is very little sun in the British Isles at that time of the year.

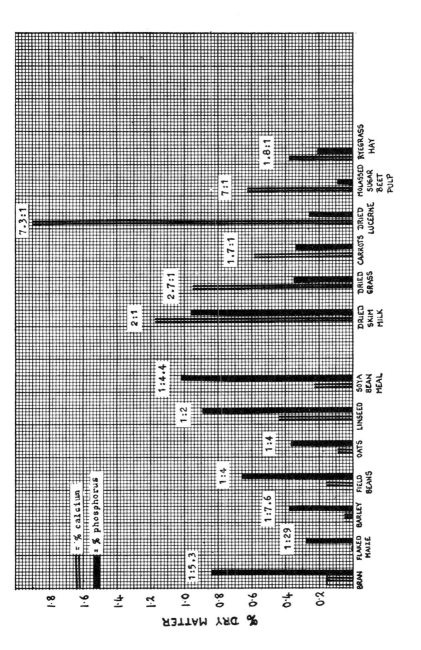

References

Hintz, H.F., Williams, A.J., Rogoff, J., and Schryver, H.F. 'Availability of phosphorus in wheat bran when fed to ponies' *J. Anim. Sci., 36*, 522-25 (1973).

Linerode, P.A., PhD., Dissertation, Ohio State University (1966).

Mansson, I. 'The intestinal flora in horses with certain skin changes' *Acta Path. Microbiol. Scand. Suppl. 119* 1-102 (1957).

Miller, R.F., PhD., 35th Minnesota Nutrition Conference (1976).

Slade, L.M., Bishop, R., Morris, J.G. and Robinson, D.W. 'Digestion and the absorption of fifteen N-labelled microbial protein in the large intestine of the horse' *Br. Vet. J., 127,* xi-xiii (1971).

Glossary and Useful Information

Ad lib feeding: the labour-saving method whereby animals eat as much and as often as they wish.

Amino acids: the 'building blocks' of which proteins are composed. There are one hundred or more known amino acids, approximately twenty-five of which are associated with proteins. Some are synthesised within the horse but ten (known as the essential amino acids) are not and therefore must be present in the food in satisfactory amounts.

Appetite: the desire to eat.
   Depraved appetite: When animals eat soil, their manes and tails or chew woodwork; it may be due to a mineral deficiency or just boredom.
   Diminished appetite (Anorexia): when animals eat less than normal, often a sign of illness.
   Excessive appetite: when animals eat more than is normal for their age, breed or the work they are doing; maybe due to disease conditions, worms or just habit.

Average standard of foodstuffs: since there are normal variations between samples of the same foodstuff, an average standard has to be taken by the various authorities. The more different foods there are in a ration the greater the chance that the various pluses and minuses in quality will cancel one another out but obviously greater care must be taken when buying a major component such as oats.

Barn hay drying: two systems of barn drying are available. In one, hay bales are stacked tightly on a false floor of weldmesh and air is blown into the enclosed chamber below the hay over a period of ten to fourteen days. In the other, a blind tunnel is constructed while building a small stack and a mobile fan is used to blow air through the bales.
   Barn drying: for this method a barn with a false floor is essential, together with a higher output fan. It is, however, possible to handle a younger crop baled at moisture levels up to 35 per cent maximum.
   Barn conditioning: this describes funnel drying or where a fan is suspended from the roof of a barn. Generally the crop is cut at the normal stage, but one day less curing in the field is possible by baling at 25-28 per cent moisture. A lower capacity fan can be used as less pressure is needed to blow the air through the bales.
   For both methods bales should be made slightly less densely compressed than normal.

Carbohydrates: organic compounds containing carbon, hydrogen and oxygen, the last two being in the same proportions as in water. The simplest are monosaccharids (e.g. glucose), then disaccharids (e.g. cane sugar), followed by the more complex compounds which include starches and cellulose.

Cellulose: the fibrous carbohydrate which forms the support structure of most plants, the proportion of which increases with the age of the plant.

Cereals: are plants of the grass family used to produce edible seeds, e.g. oats, barley, wheat and rye.

Chelates: the word 'chelate', derived from 'chela' meaning 'claw', describes the way in which a metallic ion is loosely held within an organic molecule, so preventing it from reacting adversely with other metals. Some mineral supplements are now treated with synthetic chelating agents, such as EDTA (Ethylenediaminetetracetic acid), to help improve the availability of some of the minerals. In theory, this is thought to be especially useful for diets rich in phytic acid (see page 54).

Cost per ton (tonne): this is an important factor when making up rations for farm stock but where horses and ponies are concerned the cost per ton (tonne) is, in itself, a most inadequate measure of a feed's worth; a truer measure is the horse's or pony's performance.

Daily ration: the total weight of feedingstuffs (expressed on a 12 per cent moisture basis), necessary on average, per day, to satisfy the nutritional needs of a horse or pony of a given kind.

Diet: for horses and ponies this is usually based on a mixture of:
roughage (hay, silage, etc);
cereals (including cereal by-products) e.g. oats, bran;
animal proteins (e.g. milk powder);
vegetable proteins (e.g. soya bean meal);
minerals;
vitamins.

Energy: this can be expressed in a number of different ways, e.g. digestible energy, metabolisable energy, total digestible nutrients. The total daily energy intake depends on the energy value of the foods multiplied by the amount fed.

Enzymes: organic catalysts secreted by living plants and animal cells, which have the power to change the chemical state of other substances without undergoing any change themselves.

Feed supplement: a product obtained by mixing two or more materials (usually vitamins, minerals or flavours) together to form a product normally used to supplement other foodstuffs in small quantities (less than 1/20th of the total).

Food requirement: the sum of the maintenance requirement and the production requirement.

Green crop fractionation: a new process whereby green crops (e.g. lucerne) are pulped, the juice extracted and divided from the fibre. The fibre and juice can then be used for animals with different nutritional requirements. In the future, protein may be extracted from the juice, dried and used as a valuable source of natural protein to supplement compound rations.

Growth: the rate of gain in body weight, normally most rapid between two and three months of age; growth increases the body's requirement for protein, vitamins and minerals.
Average liveweight gains in horses and ponies:

Age (months)	Mean wt. increase lb (kg)	Age (months)	Mean wt. increase lb (kg)
0– 7	504 (229)	19–24	174 (79)
8–12	328 (149)	25–30	170 (77)
13–18	220 (100)	31–36	60 (27)

(Data by kind permission of G. Hall Esq., R.H.M.).

Expeller and solvent extraction: oil seed crops were originally grown for their oil content alone but these days the residue from extraction is considered as important as the oil itself.
  Two methods are used in the manufacturing process. In the first, the seeds are heated and passed through a screw press, which expresses the oil mechanically. The residue is known as expeller cake and this is broken into kibbles the size of peas or beans. It contains 5–8 per cent oil.
  When the oil is of high value the expeller residue is extracted with solvent. To remove all the solvent after treatment, the residue is heated or 'toasted'. It then contains only ½–2 per cent oil, is richer in protein than the expeller cake but is also more dusty.
  Soya bean meal is generally only available in the extracted form. Most other protein residues can be obtained as expeller cake or extracted meal.

Hyper-: a prefix used to describe an excess of anything, e.g. hypervitaminosis – the condition caused by an excess of a vitamin. Hypo- on the other hand, means a deficiency.

Lactation: the period during which a mare gives milk. This is related directly to the rate at which milk is removed from the udder. If the demand ceases, the supply will automatically dry up. Peak lactation is believed to occur when the foal is between two and three months old, and for an average Thoroughbred mare the yield can be in the region of 35 lb (16 kg) per day. However, the ability to convert food into milk varies between individual mares and is influenced by such factors as heredity and diet. During one month at the peak of her lactation a mare will produce her own body weight in milk.
Average milk production in lb (kg)/day:

Age of foal (months)	Heavy Horse	Light Horse	Small Pony
0 – 1	34 (15)	31 (14)	23 (10.5)
1 – 2	37 (17)	32 (14.5)	26 (11.8)
2 – 3	40 (18)	37 (17)	28 (12.7)
3 – 4	37 (17)	33 (15)	21 (9.5)
4 – 5	32 (14.5)	24 (11)	20 (9)

(A gallon of milk weighs approx. 10 lb (4.5 kg).)

Lignin: the indigestible woody, fibrous material which makes up the skeleton of plants as they age. It is found mainly in the stalks.

Lysine: One of the ten essential amino acids and the one most deficient in cereals. Lysine is sometimes given as a feed supplement; it greatly improves the value of the protein in the diet but leaves methionine as the new limiting amino acid and so on, when other individual amino acids are supplied (see page 148). It is therefore better and also far cheaper to supplement the whole range of essential amino acids by using a good quality natural protein food such as soya bean or fish meal.

Maintenance requirement: the amount of food required by a horse or pony, which is not in work, growing, breeding òr lactating, to maintain its current body weight under optimum environmental conditions and includes any voluntary exercise necessary for grazing and other normal activities.

Malt: is obtained by heat treating germinated barley grains; it contains the enzyme diastase, plus malt sugar and dextrine. Diastase helps to convert dietary starch to sugar.

Milk composition:

	Water %	Protein %	Fat %	Sugar (Lactose) %	Minerals %
Mare:	90.5	2.0	1.2	5.8	0.5
Cow:	87.4	3.4	3.8	4.8	0.6
Skim milk	1.0 –	33.3 –	1.0 –	45.6 –	7.9 –
powder:	7.4	37.7	2.6	52.2	8.2
Goat:	84.2	4.0	6.0	5.0	0.8

During pregnancy the body tends to store calcium and phosphorus so that it can draw on them during lactation. Milk is notoriously deficient in other minerals so the level of these cannot be significantly raised through the mare's food; they must be made available to the foal itself. The lactating mare requires approximately twice as much energy in her diet as she did before foaling.

Moulds: small plants found in damp conditions, some of which can cause disease or produce toxins which cause disease conditions.

Mowburnt: a term used to describe over-heated hay or dried grass. The sugars tend to be oxidised and some will combine with proteins, giving the characteristic brown colour and sweet smell. Mowburnt forage has a lower nutritive value.

Phytates: substances present in cereals, particularly bran and oats, which render the phosphorus less available and lead to the formation of insoluble salts of calcium and magnesium and are therefore a potential cause of epiphysitis and other bone conditions.

Preservative: any substance which, if added to a foodstuff, delays, retards or prevents the development of rancidity or other deterioration arising from microbial activity. Experiments are currently being carried out on methods of making quality hay without barn drying. A preservative, such as ammonium dipropionate, is added to the swath before baling at the rate of 1½ gallons (6.9 litres) per ton (tonne) of hay, which can then be baled at similar moisture levels as barn dried hay. Thorough mixing of the chemical is essential to prevent mould growth. Moulds in hay are the main cause of broken-wind in horses and the toxins they produce can cause broodmares to abort. The main problem is to ensure even mixing of the preservative. Propionic acid (Propcorn) is also used to preserve both hay and grain.

Production requirement: the amount of food required by a horse or pony which is working, growing, breeding or lactating, to carry out that work or activity without altering its condition and is in addition to the maintenance requirement. It is important to ensure at all times that food is not the limiting factor to a horse's success.

Protein: organic compounds containing nitrogen in addition to carbon, hydrogen and oxygen. The amount of crude protein in a food means the amount of nitrogen multiplied by 6.25 but does not include the nitrogen present in such substances as urea, nor does it take into account the amino acid quality.

Protein equivalent of urea: the amount of urea nitrogen multiplied by 6.25.

Repletion: the feeling of fullness; adult horse's daily capacity is 2.5 per cent of body weight, youngstock and broodmares in the last 90 days of gestation and during lactation 3 per cent.

Rock salt: lumps of salt obtained from salt mines which can be used for all horses and ponies as an alternative to salt licks, but an *ad lib* supply of fresh water must be available when salt is fed.

Roughage: the fibrous part of the diet; for stabled horses this mainly comes from the hay and is necessary for normal microbial action in the large intestine.

Salt licks: moulded lumps of salt, normally placed in purpose-made holders which hang on the wall and also protect the block of salt. They can usually be obtained as plain or mineralised salt licks, the latter also contains iodine and sometimes other trace elements.

Size of feeds:

Suggested time	Quantity of total daily ration given per feed				
7 am	20%	15%	15%		15%
12 noon	–	10%	10%		20%
5 pm	80%	75%	65%	or	30%
10 pm	–	–	10%		35%

Some people prefer to give equal quantities at each feed.

Steaming-up: the practice of feeding in-foal mares a higher protein ration starting some twelve weeks before foaling to help ensure a normal size foal at birth and a maximum milk yield after foaling. A form of 'steaming-up' is also used to help barren and maiden mares conceive early in the year.

Toxins: poisons produced principally by some bacteria and moulds; many cause disease conditions and will often remain in contaminated food even after the organisms themselves have been destroyed by heat treatment.

Variations (permitted limits of, in feedingstuffs): permitted variations, either way from the stated analysis, are allowed by law and vary slightly between different foodstuffs. For example, in compound foods (nuts and cubes) the limits of variations are: oil 0.75 per cent or 1/10th of the amount stated, whichever is the greater; protein 1/10th of the amount stated; fibre, if the actual amount exceeds that stated, 0.5 per cent or 1/8th of the amount stated, whichever is the greater, of if the actual amount is less than that stated, 0.5 per cent or 1/2 of the amount stated, whichever is the greater.

Therefore, a nut with a declared 10 per cent protein level can legitimately vary between 9 and 11 per cent protein.

Units: When assessing nutrient requirements, constructing diets or comparing foods, care should be taken to check the units used. Under the MAFF Feedingstuffs Regulations, oil, protein and fibre are expressed on a fresh weight basis. For example, if a bag of horse nuts is declared to contain 15 per cent protein, this means that the nuts, as offered for sale, will contain that amount of protein.

Tables of feedingstuffs, however, may give values on a fresh weight basis, or in more recent publications, on a dry matter basis. This enables one to compare the quality of various feeds from a technical viewpoint but allowance must be made for the moisture content of each food before deciding which one is, in fact, the best commercial buy.

Tables of nutrient requirements for animals, such as the one given on page 26, are usually stated on a dry matter basis and this must be taken into account when constructing rations. If fresh weight values for, say, protein, are used in a ration calculation, the figures taken from the tables must be on a fresh weight basis. Similarly, if the requirement is quoted in terms of dry matter, the figures used for the calculation must be on a dry matter basis.

For dry foods such as hay, cereals and protein concentrates, the factor of 0.85 may be used to convert fresh weight to a dry matter (DM) basis:

e.g. % protein in DM = % protein in the fresh food ÷ 0.85;
   % protein in fresh food = 0.85 × % protein in DM;
   % protein requirement in DM × 0.85 = % protein requirement on a fresh weight basis.

In this book all figures are expressed on a dry matter basis; care should therefore be taken when using figures from other sources.

Index